Community as a Safe Place to Land

Steve Piscitelli

ISBN: 978-0-9982585-1-5
Printed in the United States
2019

First Edition

Also, by Steve Piscitelli

Stories about Teaching, Learning, and Resilience: No Need to be an Island
Choices for College Success
Study Skills: Do I Really Need This Stuff?
Engaging Activities for Student Success
I Don't Need This Stuff! Or Do I? A Study Skills and Time Management Book
Does Anyone Understand This Stuff?
A Student Guide to Organizing United States History

*Dedicated to those who work to create a
compassionate community for
consideration, conversation, and collaboration*

Contents

GRATITUDE · xi

THE MESSAGE · xvii

   Seven Core Values for Purpose and Growth · · · · · · · · · · · · xviii

EXAMINING COMMUNITY · **xxiii**

   What Does Community Mean? · · · · · · · · · · · · · · · · · · · xxiv

   Why Do We Need Community? · · · · · · · · · · · · · · · · · · · xxv

   What Factors Hinder Community Sustainability? · · · · · · · · · · xxv

   What Factors Foster Community? · · · · · · · · · · · · · · · · · xxvi

   Is a Like-minded Community Necessarily Exclusive? · · · · · · · xxviii

   How Will You Remain Vigilant? · · · · · · · · · · · · · · · · · · xxix

   A Deeper Dive: VPEER · xxx

SECTION 1: RELATIONSHIPS

The connection between two or more people, groups, processes,

ideas, or plans. · 1

   A Transformational Story about Community:

   "A Safe Place to Land." · 1

   Before You Start · 4

   1.1. When Islands Protect & Support · · · · · · · · · · · · · · · · · 6

   1.2. The Multidimensional Community: The Six Fs · · · · · · · · · · 9

   1.3. Taking Risks · 13

1.4. Vulnerability, Mistakes, & Movement Forward · · · · · · · · · · 16
1.5. Others, Optimism, & Opportunity · · · · · · · · · · · · · · · · · 19
1.6. Community Leadership · 22
1.7. Important Questions to Ask · 25
A Deeper Dive: VPEER · 29

SECTION 2: RELEVANCE
Having a connection to the issue at hand. · · · · · · · · · · · · · · · · · 31
A Transformational Story about Community:
"Trust as a Core Value." · **31**
Before You Start · 34
2.1. We Are All Related · 35
2.2. Drive Like Your Kids Live Here · · · · · · · · · · · · · · · · · · 38
2.3 Remain Relevant · 41
2.4. Core Values · 44
2.5. Change: Comprehension & Communication · · · · · · · · · · · 46
2.6. Hell, Yeah! · 49
2.7. Question Assumptions · 52
A Deeper Dive: VPEER · 55

SECTION 3: RESOURCES
Sources of support to connect and help one grow, recover,
prosper, and lend a hand. · 57
A Transformational Story about Community:
"It's Easy to be Left Behind." · **57**
Before You Start · 61
3.1. Collisions & Serendipity · 62
3.2. Come Together: Food, Friends, & Family · · · · · · · · · · · · · 65
3.3. Ask Questions · 68
3.4. On Collegiality & Caring · 71
3.5. Take Care of Your Greatest Resource · · · · · · · · · · · · · · · 74
3.6. Leadership as a Resource · 77
3.7. The Power of Networking · 80
A Deeper Dive: VPEER · 83

SECTION 4: RAINBOWS
One's dreams, goals, desires, and vision connect to one's overall journey. · · · ·85
A Transformational Story about Community:
"Mentors for Music, Hope, and Rainbows." · · · · · · · · · · · · · · ·**85**
Before You Start ·88
4.1. Where Do We Go Next? ·89
4.2. Stories You Tell Yourself ·92
4.3. Invite the Right People on Your Journey · · · · · · · · · · · · · ·96
4.4. We Can Walk a Pathway & Never See It at All · · · · · · · · · ·99
4.5. You Need to Be There, & You Need to Be There! · · · · · · · · 102
4.6. Comfort Zones: The Good & Not-So-Good · · · · · · · · · · · 107
4.7. Possibilities · 110
A Deeper Dive: VPEER · 113

SECTION 5: RESPONSIBILITY
Acting in a manner that connects to virtue and in accordance
with one's core values. · 115
A Transformational Story about Community:
"Helping a Village Find Its Voice." · · · · · · · · · · · · · · · · · ·**115**
Before You Start · 119
5.1. Priorities: Five in Your Pocket · 120
5.2. Dreams. Action. Reality! · 122
5.3. Three Ideas Worth Practicing · 125
5.4. Cogs & Linchpins · 128
5.5. Procrastination · 131
5.6. Negotiable or Non-negotiable · 134
5.7. A Post-fact World · 137
A Deeper Dive: VPEER · 140

SECTION 6: REFLECTION
Taking time to consider, ponder, remember, analyze, evaluate,
and appreciate the various connections of life. · · · · · · · · · · · · · 142
A Transformational Story about Community:
"Be the Grown Up in the Room." · · · · · · · · · · · · · · · · · · · **142**

Before You Start · 146
6.1. Words for Reflection · 148
6.2. Embrace Now · 151
6.3. Set Your Agenda · 154
6.4. A Bit Off-center · 157
6.5. Ask. Listen. Act. · 159
6.6. Past. Present. Future · 162
6.7. Choose Advisors Carefully · · · · · · · · · · · · · · · · · · 165
A Deeper Dive: VPEER · 169

SECTION 7: RESILIENCE

The ability to connect adaptability, recovery, discovery, and growth. · · · · · · 171
A Transformational Story about Community:
"Facing the Worst. Preparing for the Best." · · · · · · · · · · · · · · **171**
Before You Start · 175
7.1. A Few Thoughts and Questions about Resilience · · · · · · · · 176
7.2. HTRB as Needed · 179
7.3. On Being Responsibly Selfish · · · · · · · · · · · · · · · · · 182
7.4. Well-being Is a Skillset · 185
7.5. A Resilience Plan · 188
7.6. Meaningful Development · 191
7.7. Meaning & Authenticity · 194
A Deeper Dive: VPEER · 197

CONCLUSION: NO NEED TO BE AN ISLAND

Island: Isolated land. A place of refuge and separation. · · · · · · · · · · · · · · · · 199
Acknowledge. Anticipate. Appreciate. · · · · · · · · · · · · · · · 199
BONUS: THE SEVEN-WEEK CHALLENGE · · · · · · · · · · · · · **202**
ENDNOTES · **205**
WORKS CITED · **225**

Gratitude

❧

MOST BOOKS REFER TO THIS as the ACKNOWLEDGEMENT section. That word seems a bit distant, stodgy, and academic. Of course, I acknowledge that the following people gave me their time and feedback in the preparation of this book. More so, though, I am filled with gratitude, appreciation, and recognition of and for their efforts. Whatever you call it, the following people deserve it from me. Their help proved invaluable. Any shortcomings in this work belong to me.

Ann M. Pearson, Ashli Archer, Bobbi de Cordova-Hanks, Brittany Norris, Chris Lester, Eileen Crawford, George Maxey, Gloria Niec, Izzy Moon Mayforth, Jeannie Blaylock, Jeff Hess, Ju' Coby Pittman, Laurie Piscitelli, Linda Lanier, Marie Gnage, Marina Kaplan, Mary Pat Rosenthal, Michael Lanier, Mike *Shack* Shackelford, Preston Hodges, Jr., Reverend Billy Hester, Reverend Don R. Lynn, Sandy Golding, Thriving In Place (Celebration, FL) members, Tansy Moon, Tracy Pham.

Before you move on to the first section of the book, pause and consider how you share and show gratitude within your communities. Gratitude can manifest in any number of ways. While some may be over-the-top offerings, most come our way in simple acts of heartfelt kindness and thankfulness.

One thing I do during my morning meditations is to start with gratitude for people and other beings, opportunities, health, and experiences. This daily exercise provides gentle reminders.

How do you show gratitude? What acts of kindness have you observed or committed? Perhaps you can build upon the following ideas.

- Send a handwritten note.[1]
- Send a text message saying, "I appreciate you!" Bonus: Say why.
- Leave a voicemail.
- Volunteer.
- Put down the digital device, turn off the TV, and have a real conversation. Look into the other person's eyes.
- Pull in the neighbor's garbage can.
- Say "Thank you."
- Round up the tip for the server.
- Put out the coffee cups and spoons the night before.
- Set the table. Clear the table.
- Say "Thanks for your service" to the custodial staff at the gym, on campus, at work.
- Respond to an opposing viewpoint with grace—and seek to understand.
- Place a "Love Bucket" on your desk, in the break room, at the copy machine, or by the coffee stand for people to drop in notes of encouragement and thanks. (Note: I did this for several years in my classroom and in my office.)
- Buy the person behind you a cup of coffee.

On Facebook, I posed the question, "What simple acts of gratitude have you shown, been a recipient of, or witnessed?" Some of the responses included:

- Wrote a thank you note to a parent volunteer.
- Was in the hospital and got handmade get-well cards from over 200 students...made my day.

- A friend took me aside at a large event to tell me she had had the best afternoon reflecting on my family photos I had posted over the years on Facebook. I was so touched by her care for me.
- Hubby stopped and said thank you the other night to a doctor who stayed late and helped with testing.
- My ex-husband passed, and friends did a fundraiser for my kids.
- Perfect strangers stepping up to walk my dogs and bring me food while I was seriously ill in the hospital.
- When we were homeless, a student who knew of my situation gave me the money to pay for my hotel room for one night.
- "Good Wishes" jar from my students in a recent course.
- Sweetest Mother's Day card ever from a son who obviously "gets it" and appreciates it!
- A handwritten Mother's Day letter from my 11-year old son that incorporates his English class skills!
- Received a handmade Mother's Day card from a girl I babysit.
- In the hospital, in a lot of pain and scared … was wheeled back to my room and saw two precious therapy dogs and their copilots! Made my day.
- Gave a shout out to my network to recommend a colleague for their excellent service.
- Took in some elderly people's garbage cans for them.
- We helped somebody dock [their boat] while it was pouring. They gave us about five bags of groceries.
- When my dad died …three of my [former] students offered to clean up, so I could be with my mom and siblings. When I came home, there were fresh flowers and a cooked meal for us!

About the Author

❧

Hi, I'm Steve.

Truth be told, you could have written this book, or at least a version of it. All of us have lived in communities of one form or another. And based on those experiences, we gather observations—remarkable as well as ordinary. When we stop, think, and appreciate how our communities have imprinted themselves on our own development, the ordinary can easily become remarkable

This book represents a few observations I have made during my journey through and as a part of various communities. My communities have included classroom teaching, conference and workshop facilitations, songwriting and music recording, video production, writing and publishing, podcasting, pet therapy, local event development, friendships, sports fans, the local gym, beach walkers and kayakers, faith-based groups, intellectual discussion groups, and friends gathering for benchmark celebrations.

I bring, among others, the following perspectives to this work:

* Classroom teacher for thirty-three years;
* National speaker and workshop facilitator for more than two decades;
* A neighbor and community volunteer;
* A husband for more than 40 years;
* An ongoing student of life;

- A friend;
- An author of 12 books, a weekly blog, and a podcast channel;
- Songwriter with two full-length original music CDs;
- A pet therapy team member (along with my wonder dog, Roxie, who is really the team leader); and
- An only child who, early in life, sought to find a safe place to land.

Thank you for allowing me to facilitate the following community-building journey with you.

The Message

The ache for home lives in all of us,
the safe place where we can go as we are and not be questioned.

—ATTRIBUTED TO MAYA ANGELOU

Thank you for choosing this book.

In 2017, I wrote *Stories about Teaching, Learning, and Resilience: No Need to be an Island* to explore the power of collaboration, mindfulness, and resilience in higher education. I dedicated that volume to college and university faculty and administrators. Thirty-seven scenarios, inspired by actual teaching and learning issues and events, guided the readers on a thoughtful journey of consideration, conversation, and collaboration.

This volume continues the community-building journey and expands beyond the college teaching and learning dynamic. This book will allow you and your network(s) to explore the concept of community on a wider scale. For you, community might conjure up civic organizations, residential neighborhoods, politically oriented groups, a book club, your workplace, a department within your workplace, or college co-curricular clubs. Others might connect community to the gym, yoga studio, a jogging club, or a long-distance biking group.

Regardless of the location or makeup, with this book we will examine what builds community and what breaks it apart. And, how at its heart, community is about providing a safe place for its members to explore, learn, fail, and grow.

Rather than creative scenarios, though, this book pulls from my blog posts on www.*TheGrowthandResilienceNetwork.net*. When I started the blog in the spring of 2010, I wanted to share uplifting and practical messages about growth and resilience. The posts have explored what brings us together, what may separate us, and how we can focus on movement to improvement for ourselves and those with whom we lead, mentor, and collaborate. You will find pertinent community-based lessons.

Seven Core Values for Purpose and Growth

A vibrant, communicative, and respectful community builds its strength and cohesion on solid core values. Each community needs to identify, discuss, commit to, and live according to its recognized values. Over the life of my blog, seven values repeated themselves.

As I researched, shared, observed, and traveled, I came to understand that any healthy and vibrant community considers each of these values at some level or another. As you study each, consider how communication and respect form a foundation. When engaged in transparent and civil conversation, purposeful communities allow us to:

* Surround ourselves with respectful **RELATIONSHIPS** that help us grow as people and a team;
* Discover and use **RESOURCES** to increase chances for progress, growth, learning, and connections;
* Evaluate experiences for their **RELEVANCE** to community growth;
* Give voice to our **RAINBOWS**—our dreams and aspirations— and take action to move toward them;
* Set aside time for frequent **REFLECTION** about what we do, why we do it, and adjustments we may need to make. We remain curious;
* Act with **RESPONSIBILITY** toward others and ourselves; and
* Pay attention and foster self-care and **RESILIENCE**.

The Seven Rs form the nexus of networks and support systems. Struggling communities more than likely come up short on one or more of the core values.

I developed my Rs while teaching college-level student success classes and preparing for my national speaking engagements. I started with three Rs: Relevance, Relationships, and Rainbows[2]. The rest evolved organically as I reviewed the literature on student success, followed my passion, my calling, and my students' lead in the classroom. I paid attention to what I was doing, saying, reading, observing, hearing, and practicing.[3]

The lessons in this book demonstrate how each of the seven core values contribute to personal and community growth and resilience. Whether you talk about your neighborhood, your workplace, your family, or some other vital group in your life, thriving communities focus on developing each of The Seven Rs.

A functioning community, though, must go beyond listing and reciting core values. How does your community *share* and *live* its values? What about differences of opinion? Does the environment—the atmosphere—of the community allow people to speak what's on their minds? Can they share their vulnerabilities without fear of chastisement or marginalization?

Community building requires both communication and respect. What passes for communication can end up little more than pontification, self-congratulation, and agenda-promoting if the members do not listen and value the input from one another. We can talk all we want about shared vision. Without compassion and transparent communication, however, such a goal is illusory at best.

It's easy to have a conversation when we speak with those with whom we agree. It becomes difficult when the other party, or we, believe nothing can be learned from our disagreements and continued dialogue. In those situations, we tend to *tune out* the other party.

Energy practitioners believe the fifth energy chakra—the Throat chakra—connects to a clear voice; integrity of message. It is associated with the sense of hearing. To have a clear and authentic message, we need to hear what the other person, group, and ideologues say. That requires acts of listening, not commissions of me-centered statements. Listening creates the foundation for respect. The Seven Rs lose potency without respectful communication.

To help you apply this model, I divided this book into seven sections—one R (one core value) per section. Each begins with a thought about how adherence to that principle builds or sustains community. Next, you will read a transformational story about how one community exemplifies that core value.

The remaining pages of each section provide excerpts from seven selected blog posts that connect that core value to community growth and resilience. A citation will lead you to the full blog post for further illustration.

The process of community building is ongoing. You may find hidden truths by examining the present, looking to the past, and gazing into the future. What tried and true resources and insights will your community need to recognize to sustain itself going into the future? And what processes may be tired and in need of revision or elimination?

As you work through this book, consider the seven core values as interlocking pieces for future-focused community growth and resilience. This book is for and about your communities' well-being. The highlighted transformational communities that appear in these pages, as well as the illustrative blog posts, serve as tools.

I envision small community groups reading and then discussing, debating, and digesting the subject matter as it pertains to their respective needs. Make the material personal and the follow-up conversations authentic. Take three basic steps:

- **Consideration**: Read each post;
- **Conversation**: Discuss the post and your insights with others in your community. Agree. Disagree. Listen. Question. Learn. Change. Grow. Repeat; and
- **Collaboration**: Create a plan of action.

Finally, I do not present the order of the material as *THE* way to go. Consider the Table of Contents as a starting point for further dialogue. If your team is struggling with one of the core values, you may benefit from jumping into the book at that point.

I hope this book will become the go-to resource for your community-building and community-sustaining conversations.

And remember, there is no need to be an island.

—Steve Piscitelli
The Growth and Resilience Network®
Atlantic Beach, Florida
2019

Examining Community

BEFORE YOU DIG INTO THE core values, stories, and blog excerpts, you would do well to pause and reflect on the term *community*. Since it is the focus of this book, let's discuss what it means—and may not mean.

We hear, see, experience, and read about divisiveness on a regular basis. Network and cable news. Breaking news alerts on your tablet and smartphone. Clashing protestors. Loud voices getting louder. Common ground seems difficult to reach with the shouting voices, pointing fingers, and mean-spirited attacks. Fear, disgust, and mistrust carry the day. A lot of *us, good* and *them, bad* thinking. When dialogues devolve into collective monologues, we miss out on our shared identity.

Lost in shouting, apprehension, and suspicion will be the potential for respectful relationships, diverse and inclusive communication, and the power of responsible reflection to nourish resilience.

An internet search[4] for the term *community* turned up millions upon millions of hits. Whether providing people in distress a comfortable place to land, transporting a neighbor to a doctor's appointment, running errands for a homebound couple, or helping someone find a seat for dinner, people reach out and seek conversation, comfort, and connection. The community spirit lives.

If you can facilitate a conversation about community, consider four questions for a starting point:

* What does community mean?
* Why do we need community?

- If you had to name ONE action that HINDERS or even destroys community, what comes to mind? and
- If you had to name ONE action that FOSTERS community, what comes to mind?

What Does Community Mean?[5]

What does community mean to you? Does it conjure up a definition? Or does it bring about a feeling? Do your communities consist of like-minded people and do they demonstrate inclusiveness? Does community exist as a concept any longer? Or does the traditional concept need a transformation to reflect where we stand now, and more importantly, what the future holds?

Definitions of *community* include the concepts of *inclusion, a sense of caring, respectful relationships, belonging, network, care, concern, support, encouragement, familiarity, ties, like-minded people,* and *commonality.*

A community cooperates, shares, and helps its members grow. We can belong to several different communities both personally and professionally. Community can refer to your family, neighborhood, town, corporate department, religious organization, youth group, athletic team, exercise partners, or project collaborators. Your personal communities can include locations like the neighborhood where you live, your place of worship, your fitness center, a café, school events, sporting contests, and volunteer opportunities.

Professional communities can develop in the employee lunch room, hiring committees, conferences and workshops, classrooms, boardrooms, labor unions, professional associations, and mentoring circles.

Healthy communities surround us. They can help us grow.

And for those of us in less-than-optimal environments—where community has been challenged on one or more levels—we might need to focus on small steps we can take to establish feelings of inclusion, respect, and concern. Who can help us take those initial steps?

WHY DO WE NEED COMMUNITY?

Dan Buettner, a longevity researcher and founder of *Blue Zones*, pointedly and unequivocally writes "of all the things people can do to try to increase their happiness, the most effective and lasting one is to choose to live in a community that supports well-being….You can't do it on your own….You can redirect your life toward greater happiness and well-being only when the world you live in supports you."[6]

In his groundbreaking book, *Anatomy of an Illness as Perceived by the Patient*, Norman Cousins offered that "Complete retirement from active life does not seem to be a very good way to reach a very old age."[7]

As you will read in each of the seven transformational stories in this book, social networks create pathways for agency. Whether we talk about a church's resurrection, a community reaching out to its aging population, forming a breast cancer support group, or addressing neighborhood health and access disparities, social capital nurtures growth and well-being. Perhaps, at its core, we require community to satisfy a need to connect with other souls.

The question, in my mind, moves beyond *why* we need community to *how* we go about building and sustaining it.

WHAT FACTORS HINDER COMMUNITY SUSTAINABILITY?

Factors that block, slow, or hinder community building and sustainability may include *exclusion, cliques, time demands, architectural designs, mean-spirited conflict, competing goals, divisiveness, selfishness, fear mongering, hate,* and *closing one's mind to the ideas of others.*

The metaphor of silos comes to mind. They exist on college campuses and in the corporate setting. When silos of separation become entrenched, it becomes harder to construct bridges of collaboration.

All professions and callings tend to reference their *best practices.* These are the *tried and true* actions, strategies, and techniques that have been used over and repeatedly. Ad nauseam. After a while they cease to be questioned. They are considered sacrosanct. Introduction of new ideas or methods can easily be met with "That's not how we do things around here!"

Unfortunately, without due diligence, these *best practices* can become *tired.*

As you read the following pages, I suggest you question all *best practices* regarding community. Hold them suspect. At the least, you and your community builders need to be skeptical (not cynical) of accepting them just because "that's how we do things around here." It might be that "that's how we do it around here" because it is effective. Or it could be you have gone on autopilot and have failed to ask needed questions. At least, be aware of assumptions and have a conversation about your practices.

In their work *Preparing for a Future that Doesn't Exist—Yet,* Rick Smyre and Neil Richardson urge us "to find connections where none apparently exist from a traditional perspective. We need to look for potential impacts of 'weak signals' (what we call early signs of change) before they create crisis."[8]

Einstein warned us, "If you continue doing what you've always done, you will always get what you always got."

Consider what would transpire if you never change what you do for your community or never take steps to question current practices. Eventually, what you always got will no longer be good enough. What would have happened—what would you have missed—if you had insisted on keeping and re-adjusting those *rabbit ears* on top of your analogue television? After all, they always worked in the past. In fact, think of most technological advancements. While there is a learning curve and a time of dis-ease and discomfort, embracing the change brought about new possibilities (and challenges, as well). Each change offers an opportunity for a community to examine itself, make needed adjustments, and sustain its growth.

What Factors Foster Community?[9]

Before you can move toward solutions and strategies to foster community, your community members will do well to identify those promising or emergent practices that have a chance to enhance capacity for growth and prosperity.

Community represents an emotional commitment to a group of people. It can be in a physical location or it can be virtual. Something binds the group.

One member of my music community shared,[10]

"Community is a word I think a lot about. I grew up in a 'neighborhood.' I knew every one of my neighbors. Today I live in a gated 'community.' I know nearly no one. Community has to be more than a marketing term. It's an expression of true care and concern for others. Actions and deeds. Not words or labels."

We can build community on the front porch, in the workplace, at a place of worship, around the neighborhood, and even in a gated-community. Communities can grow when their members gather in specific locations, participate, act with selflessness, build trust, and openly communicate. Community leaders attempt to have discussions (difficult discussions) about shared values as well as conflicting values.

Strength, evolution, and depth of community also depends on how well we pay attention to signals indicating that the way of the past is not necessarily the way of the future. You will find value in examining how to move from clinging to past practices to envisioning what the future holds. How will you go beyond relying on historically-based best practices to promising and emerging future-focused practices? As the world continues to change and make seismic shifts, futurists tell us "we need to find connections where none apparently exist from a traditional perspective. We need to look for potential impacts of weak signals (what we call *early* signs of change) before they create a crisis...we need to change the very nature of the questions we ask."[11]

Community building requires more than just living near one another.

IS A LIKE-MINDED COMMUNITY NECESSARILY EXCLUSIVE?

Terms such as *inclusive, like-minded,* and *diverse* often describe the concept of community. Perhaps examining these concepts as they relate to your community would be helpful. Consider the following intellectual engagement.

If we surround ourselves with a community of people who believe as we do (politically, socially, nutritionally, economically, or religiously) can it be inclusive? Or, because we live in a diverse community (politically, socially, nutritionally, economically, or religiously) does that make it inclusive? And if it is inclusive, can it be a gathering of like-minded individuals? Or do we, within a community, still segregate ourselves into smaller like-minded groupings—smaller like-minded sub-communities? Is inclusiveness an idealized goal within a diverse community?

Or as one reviewer of this book offered, "Inclusivity is the practice of including people beyond comfort or like-ness. The only like-mindedness of inclusive folks is to be open to others."[12]

We can argue that most groupings, a workplace for instance, have diversity below the surface beyond race, ethnicity, age, or gender. Differences exist of generation, schooling (duration, types, and location), residence, family situation, musical tastes, news source preferences, wealth accumulation, health, fitness levels, nutritional habits, music tastes, recreational preferences, and more. We might not see those when we walk around the company campus, yet they are there and have an impact on the community.

But *saying* we are inclusive and diverse and *living* it can be two different sides of the coin. Has your community discussed this aspect of belonging?

The above questions will generate conversation and deeper questions that have meaning to your communities. The Seven Rs and the pages that follow will guide you.

How Will You Remain Vigilant?

Have you ever been part of a community that appeared to be stagnating? To outside observers, the challenges would have been imperceptible. But to you, signs popped up. Some minor irritants, perhaps, while others loomed as storm clouds. The challenges could have come from sinister outside forces. Or, the erosion of community may have been the result of an internal complacency. The members became *comfortable* and *took for granted* their community would always be there.

As an example, colleges and universities invest a great deal in recruiting and retaining first-year students. They offer orientations, first-year experience success courses, dedicated counselors, and residences halls. Each strategy has the goal of helping the students to build community, feel comfortable in that community, and return to that community for their second year of college.

But what happens the second year, third year, and beyond? Will resources be invested to *re-recruit* the students—to keep the idea of the college community foremost in their minds? How will community be sustained? Will core values change? Will *best practices* continue to work?

Consider a workplace that invests hundreds of staff hours in screening and interviewing candidates for a position. Perhaps there is an orientation of sorts. What happens to the new employee after that? Is the new person greeted with one mind-numbing bureaucratic checklist after another, or does she receive a meaningful welcome that recognizes and nurtures the powerful transition to her new community? As the Heath brothers pointed out in *The Power of Moments*, "What a wasted opportunity [not] to make a new team member feel included and appreciated. Imagine if you treated a first date like a new employee."[13]

A Deeper Dive: VPEER[14]

A vigilant community deepens and develops capacities for sharing, cooperating, and growing. This five-step model provides a process for reflection and growth. At the end of each of the book's sections you will be encouraged to apply these concepts to your community. You and your community members will consider how to:

- **Visualize** the purpose, journey, and membership of your community. What signals, signs, or patterns exist to indicate the future of your community will not look like the past? What does this future focus tell you? What does the community you envision look like?

- **Prioritize** the resources you will need and the actions required to sustain your community—and make it thrive into the future. What non-negotiable steps do you need to take? What comes first? How will you prioritize the core value (the R) presented in each section?

- **Exorcise** those forces that no longer serve or nourish your community. How can you minimize or eliminate their pernicious effects? Where does this fit with your prioritization of resources and actions? Who will help you identify these factors? Where will this fit in your prioritization?

- **Exercise** and strengthen the emotional, physical, and spiritual dimensions of life. Community building can be challenging work. How will you and your members build and maintain a healthy lifestyle moving forward? Where can you find this on your list of priorities?

- **Realize** your visualization. How often will you stop to evaluate your progress? How will you realize if you are faithfully following the four steps above (visualize, prioritize, exorcise, and exercise) and if you need to make detours?

A FINAL REMINDER FOR USING THIS BOOK.

Rather than develop and refine your thoughts about your community (the group) in isolation, work and grow with others. Form a reading group to scrutinize, apply, and develop the concepts found in the following pages. Discuss, fine-tune, and practice the book's concepts as they relate to your community. One size does not fit all. The following pages provide a starting point for agreement and respectful disagreement. Communicate your insights, interpretations, and inquiries as you develop and apply the concepts of inclusion, respect, support, belonging, network, and encouragement. Communication assumes listening, adjusting, refining, sharing, and growth.

Have authentic conversations by practicing consideration, conversation, and collaboration. When we do this, we come to understand the value of having a safe place to land.

Relationships

The connection between two or more people, groups, processes, ideas, or plans.

❦

RELATED TERMS INCLUDE: CIVILITY, CRITICAL thinking, communication, collaboration, community, core values, gratitude, inspiration, integrity, leadership, legacy, mentorship, and *respect.*[15]

A TRANSFORMATIONAL STORY ABOUT COMMUNITY: "A SAFE PLACE TO LAND"[16]

Consider this. It's 1993. You are an exuberant minister with a young and growing family. You walk into a church in a high crime-high poverty part of a Southern city. The congregation has dwindled to about 25 souls, most hovering near 80 years of age. The church cannot afford to pay you a full salary.

What do you do?

Well, if you were the Reverend Billy Hester, you step into the sanctuary and lead the resurrection of a dying and still proud church. Twenty-five years later (2018), Billy (as he is fondly and commonly known in the area) and that same church boast a vibrant congregation of 650 diverse, committed, supportive souls. On Sundays, you'll find packed pews in the Asbury Memorial United Methodist Church.[17] So, what made the difference between shuttering and growing the church? What fueled the resilience?

Billy and his Lay Leader, Preston Hodges, Jr., sat with me in a church conference room in Savannah, Georgia, and helped me understand how Asbury came to be such a caring and vibrant community. While the importance of a focused and transformational leader cannot be overstated, I kept hearing about the connections between congregants and neighborhood, congregants and congregants, as well as congregants and their own selves. This spiritual community thrives because of its foundational values. As you read each value below, consider the connection to The Seven Rs as well.

* **Acceptance and Authenticity.**
  * When you walk in the door, you do not have to pretend to be what you are not. You do not have to hide who you are. Billy explained the concept of *koinonia*: fellowship, participation, sharing, and contribution. One parishioner, according to Preston, said she found "A loving, open and accepting Church that includes all of us — as Jesus would — with love, without judgment....You're always welcome!" Inclusion. Or, simply, community. Another former parishioner shared what Asbury did for her in a difficult time: "That congregation of loving and accepting people tied a knot at the end of my rope so that I could hang on."
* **Listening and Reflection.**
  * The words "I don't know" play an important part at Asbury. The congregants remain free to explore (are encouraged to explore) their own paths. Rather than a church that remains stagnant, dogmatic, and unquestioning, the members find encouragement to question and admit when they do not know something. And then search for the answers. To communicate we must first listen—truly listen—to one another. Then we connect and appreciate.
* **Vulnerability and Growth.**
  * When we let go of the need to be *right* at all costs and the need to cling to unaccepting dogma, we open to vulnerability[18]—and

growth opportunities. There will be times when people disappoint us. And when that happens, the congregation has made the commitment to hang in there "until grace happens." But, someone may draw within *and* withdraw from the church. If someone *goes missing*, church members notice and reach out to make sure all is OK. They refer to the non-intrusive practice as "Calling the Missing."

* **Relevance and Resilience.**
  * Billy's sermons must pass a two-part litmus test. (1) Do the words connect with people by helping them identify with the message? (2) What is the positive impact of this message on the listeners' lives? Again, it's not about showing how much the preacher knows about content. Rather, how does the content help people accept, live, and grow together as a community?
  * In 2014, The Pastoral Parish Committee and Church Council concluded that Billy needed more than normal vacation time to remain fresh and vibrant for the congregation. What evolved was Seven Sundays of Sabbatical. The church gave Billy seven consecutive Sundays *off* from delivering his sermons. In his absence, Billy invites guest speakers to deliver their sermons and teach the congregation. This showed that Billy was comfortable in *his* own skin and welcomed outsiders to stand in his Sunday spot in the pulpit. These visiting speakers and their messages have rejuvenated both the reverend and the congregation.

Our conversation had many takeaways. I will leave you with one powerful observation a congregant shared with Preston and Billy.

About 35% of the Asbury congregation come from the lesbian, gay, bisexual, and transgender (LGBT) community. For most, church before Asbury's resurrection meant hiding identity. Not so any longer. The congregant[19] said Asbury has become a "safe place to land" for her and so many other congregants.

What a powerful way to describe community.

Before You Start

❦

CONSIDER COMMUNITIES—VIBRANT AS WELL AS those that struggle—to which you belong. How do RELATIONSHIPS help the vibrant ones prosper and the struggling ones grow or stagnate? What do your communities do to create a "safe place to land" for its members?

For instance, think of a dynamic community to which you belong. In what ways do the **RELATIONSHIPS** in that community contribute to its growth and resilience? How do the people and connections provide solace, caring, concern, and encouragement? Conversely, what do your struggling communities lack when it comes to **RELATIONSHIPS**?

As you read the following pages, consider how the relationships in your community have helped you and your network flourish. Who have helped the community recognize its power and uniqueness? How have the **RELATIONSHIPS** helped make your community a welcoming place for all to live? If you could improve one facet of the **RELATIONSHIPS** in your community, what would that be—and why?

Below you will find seven blog post excerpts related to the concept of **RELATIONSHIPS**. Choose one, read it, and consider its message. You will probably note that more than one of the other Seven Rs come into play as well. These core values mutually reinforce one another. Begin a conversation about **RELATIONSHIPS** and use the thoughts to foster and sustain community. Then, repeat with the other blog excerpts.

After each excerpt, you will find several suggestions and specific questions on how to bring the teachings of the piece to life in your community. Rather than settling for general answers, use the following three step model to help you be more actionable with your responses:

1. Establish a realistic, feasible, time-bound plan for implementing your proposed actions;
2. Execute your plan. Make sure all involved understand their roles and responsibilities; and
3. Evaluate your progress on a regular basis. Adjust course as needed.

When Islands Protect & Support[20]

❧

*This country will not be a good place for any of us to live in
unless we make it a good place for all of us to live in.*

— ATTRIBUTED TO TEDDY ROOSEVELT

TWO STORIES. ONE LESSON.

In 2017, my wife and I toured the Center for Civil and Human Rights in Atlanta.[21] We sat at one exhibit that replicates a lunch counter sit-in. With our hands placed on the countertop, headphones transported us to the 1960s. To a time when people took a seat to make a stand about racial prejudice and discrimination.

We sat listening to the hate-filled voices whispering—and then yelling—in our ears. They hurled threats. We heard thumps, bangs, and loud noises. At one point, we both jumped a bit from our seats at the counter. While we were never in any physical danger, we felt fearful. To say the exhibit moved us remains a gross understatement.

Within two minutes, our *demonstration* ended. The docent handed me a tissue. I dabbed my eyes, moved by the experience. I remember words attributed to MLK, Jr.: "Faith is taking the first step even when you don't see the whole staircase."

Those young 1960s protesters came together, tired of being adrift in sea of hatred. They might have been on an island, but they came together on that island and led the way.

A few days after our sit-in experience, we drove to the other end of Georgia to take part in the annual Valentine's Day Renewal of Marriage Vows in Savannah's City Market. We have participated in the yearly event since the late 1990s. The Reverend Billy Hester and his wife, Cheri, officiate. The Hesters have led the Asbury Memorial United Methodist Church[22] congregation since the early 1990s. As presented in this section's "Transformational Story," when they arrived, the church was by all appearances on its last legs.

Today the pews are full. Hundreds of people gather for praise and glory. Why? The stewardship of Hester and his wife. The inclusive nature of their authentically positive message resonated with the surrounding neighborhood. They held a lamp of humanity for many who felt alone. Each member of that congregation helps build a resilient community

They helped create a community of souls, so that individual souls would not have to struggle on their own islands.

Both stories show the power of a community coming together for protection and support, and the power of authentic relationships. These groups believe in collaboration, growth, and resilience.

Reaching out and helping each member recognize and build his and her own capacity for growth and change energizes the entire community.

The church congregation and the museum remind us of the value of coming together, appreciating, and respecting (accepting and not simply tolerating) our neighbors.

> What counts in life is not the mere fact that we have lived.
> It is what difference we have made to the lives of others.

— ATTRIBUTED TO NELSON MANDELA

Consideration, Conversation, & Collaboration

⁕ What do the productive leaders in your communities do to build capacities for growth and change? How do they work with other members?

⁕ If you are the community leader, or if you aspire to be a community leader, what three personal characteristics do you want to develop and strengthen?

⁕ List two or three community leaders you know who you hold as exemplars of building relationships. Why do these people stand out for you?

⁕ What do you do to build authentic relationships in your community?

⁕ What other questions do you need to address regarding this topic?

The Multidimensional Community: The Six Fs[23]

❧

ALL OF US ARE MULTI-DIMENSIONAL beings. One well-being model divides our lives into six dimensions[24] of social, occupational, spiritual, physical, intellectual, and emotional. When one dimension goes off the rails, it affects the others.

Consider my Six Fs: fitness, friends, family, function, finances, and faith.

All of us have experienced times when one or more of the slices, sectors, segments, or spaces of our lives do not seem to be working any longer. Something no longer serves us, no longer sustains our well-being. Once aware of the culprit, we can work to minimize or remove it.

When we identify what no longer nourishes us, and might even be debilitating us, we need to consider what to bring in as a replacement. Or more simply: Once we *make* space in a dimension of life, what can we fill that space with to nourish and serve us? What can we add to our lives to help us lead a life of meaning, purpose, and virtue?

Or maybe, once we make the space, it might be beneficial to leave the space be for a time. We might want to not fill it for the sake of filling it. Rather, we should be mindful about what we focus on, reflect on the space, and just be.

How can you use this strategy of removing, replacing, and reflecting as you consider your personal goals? For instance, using the Six Fs Model above:

* Fitness
    * What is no longer serving you well when it comes to your physical and emotional fitness? What can you, or do you need to, minimize or eliminate this from your life because it no longer serves and nourishes you?
    * Once you have made this space, how can you fill it? What new, virtuous habit can you build that will serve and nourish you?
* Friends
    * What or who is no longer serving you well when it comes to your friends? What can you, or do you need to, minimize or eliminate this relationship in your life because it no longer serves and nourishes you? This does not have to mean you are walking away from your friends. Maybe you need to make small adjustments at first. Don't forget to evaluate your own behavior, as well. You may identify a habit of yours that no longer sustains your social circle.
    * Once you have made this space, how can you fill it? What new habit or social relationship can you build that will serve and nourish those around you and yourself?
* Family
    * What is no longer serving you well when it comes to your family relationships? What can you, or do you need to, minimize or eliminate from your life because it no longer serves to nourish your family? This does not have to mean you are walking away from your family. You could identify a habit you have that is no longer serving your family unit.
    * Once you have made this space, how can you fill it? What new, virtuous habit can you build that will serve and nourish you and your family unit?

- Function
  - What is no longer serving you well when it comes to the purpose of what you do for your career, community, or clan? What can you, or do you need to, minimize or eliminate from your life because it no longer serves and nourishes your purpose? What have you been doing that denies who you are?
  - Once you have made this space, how can you fill it? What new virtuous habit can you build that will serve and nourish your sense of self?
- Finances
  - What is no longer serving you well when it comes to your financial picture? What can you, or do you need to, minimize or eliminate this practice from your life because it no longer serves to nourish your financial security? What have you been doing that jeopardizes your financial future?
  - Once you have made this space, how can you fill it? What new, virtuous habit can you build that will serve and nourish your financial future?
- Faith
  - What is no longer serving you when it comes to your religion or spirituality? What can you, or do you need to, minimize or eliminate this from your life because it no longer serves and nourishes you in this dimension?
  - Once you have made this space, how can you fill it? What new, virtuous habit can you build that will serve and nourish your sense of self?

Be mindful of the spaces in your life. All the slices, sectors, segments, or spaces make a whole you.

Consideration, Conversation, & Collaboration

❦

- First, complete the exercise above and apply the Six F model to your life. Give yourself the luxury of quality reflection time.
- Your next step is to apply the model to one of your communities. What dimension has toxic influences that need to be minimized or eliminated? Which dimension has healthy characteristics that need to be strengthened and enhanced?
- Ask a few community members to complete the same exercises independently. Compare your responses. What insights and conclusions can you draw? What questions do you still need to ponder? Next steps?
- What other questions do you need to address regarding this topic?

Taking Risks[25]

❦

TAKE A MOMENT AND WRITE four or five names of the most remarkable (in a good way) supervisors with whom you have worked. Next to each name, write why they stand out for you. What did they do that separated them from the others?

When I look at my list, each leader knew how to empower me. They did not micro-manage my every move. Trust existed. They had passion and purpose for our mission. Mostly, each one of these people knew how to focus on the needs of their followers. And we gladly followed. Together, we made a difference.

Transformational leaders[26] revolutionize our workplaces, communities, and our lives into empowerment zones. They respect and nurture us. Harvard professor Linda Hill has shared that transformational leaders know how to *set the stage*—and then let their followers become the performers. They recognize that the workplace is not about the leader but rather the "collective genius"[27] coming from team members.

The antithesis of transformational leadership is transactional leadership. These people narrowly focus on tasks—the *what* and the *how*; and they must maintain control of most aspects of the day-to-day operations. Tony Schwartz[28] warns that "if your manager knows what you're doing all the time, you're not doing your job, and neither is he."

Author and marketing strategist Seth Godin, in his book *Leap First: Creating Work that Matters*, encourages us to envision two lines, one horizontal and one vertical (each a continuum). On the left end of the horizontal line write the word *timid* (shy; reticent; fearful); and on the far right you jot the word *reckless* (careless; lack of caution; foolhardy). Label the upper end of the vertical axis *tight* (prepared; rehearsed) and the bottom end, *loose* (ill-prepared; wing it).[29]

Transformational leaders help move their followers into the upper right quadrant: prepared to take risks. "Act!" "Failure is an option." These must be more than meaningless words. Growth does not come to the timid, let's-fly-under-the-radar worker (the type of environment created by transactional leaders). Transformational leaders help followers grow. They want nothing more than personal growth and resilience for their colleagues. These leaders encourage team members to develop their own unique voices and stories.

Consideration, Conversation, & Collaboration

❧

- Use the brief video "Five Characteristics of an Effective Leader"[30] as a conversation starter. Would you drop any of these top five? If so, what characteristics would replace those?
- Which leader would you rather work for, the transformational or transactional? Why?
- Which leaders have you worked for? Relate a story about these leaders that left a memorable impression on your development.
- Which leader do you want to be remembered as?
- How does your community go about choosing its leaders? Is the process effective?
- What other questions do you need to address regarding this topic?

Vulnerability, Mistakes, & Movement Forward[31]

❧

BACK IN 2008, I SELECTED five of my recorded songs, had them burned to a *best-of* disc for marketing purposes, and then sent copies to selected colleges and corporations. I titled the CD *"Be Brief, Be Bright, Be Gone. Energize Your Next Meeting."* The studio burned 100 discs and printed the accompanying case and artwork.

Feeling proud, I showed my musical marketing tool to a colleague. She smiled and then asked,

"What's *Engergize?*"

"Oh," I said a bit confused, "You mean *Energize.*"

"No, right here, it says *Engergize,"* as she pointed to the CD cover.

My heart sank as I looked at the spelling error. In the title of the CD. That I had already sent out to university and corporate leaders.

The CD had been reviewed by three sets of eyeballs and still the mistake reared its ugly, misspelled head.

Are you kidding me?

Fast forward to a newsletter I sent to my subscriber list several years later. Again, this was reviewed probably four or five times. Once it "went live" I saw it—the grammatical error. In the *first line* of the newsletter.

Are you freaking kidding me?

I immediately started to beat myself up about it. My bride did what she could to calm me, but I persisted in the self-flagellation. Finally, I took a walk with my dog, Roxie, BDE (Best Dog Ever).

"Look," Roxie said to me with those big brown eyes, *"you made a mistake. Look at the big picture. You just sent out a newsletter with 20 free resources relating to growth and resilience. If someone gets whacked about a small error and does not even see the good stuff you provided, then maybe you don't need that unforgiving person on your list."*

Point well-taken. There are people who live to tell everyone else what they did wrong while they remain in their safely constructed cocoon.

Accepting mistakes does not mean we condone sloppy work. And certainly, some mistakes can be deadly, literally. My guess is that what most of us engage in each day would not fall into the *deadly* category. Perhaps embarrassing, awkward, or *humbling.* But not deadly.

During my tenure as a classroom teacher, I frequently encountered students so anchored to external measure of their *worth* (like their grade point average) that they refused to do anything that could result in a grade of less than 4.0. It didn't matter what they learned or even if they learned. The all-important measure was the grade. That represented self-worth. Anything short of that *A* they deemed a failure. And, *failure* was never acceptable in their eyes. Risk, vulnerability, and failure in their eyes could never lead to success. They did not stretch themselves.

And it's not just the students. Plenty of so-called leaders will not accept anything that may smack of imperfection or weakness. In their view, a mistake equates with deficiency, failing, and ineptitude. The transformational leaders encourage their followers to fail, learn, and grow.[32] They understand.

Selfies scream, "Look at how unique I am!" Have we moved to a space that "fears being ordinary"[33] today?

Acknowledge, take ownership of, and grow from your mistakes and you will not be ordinary.

Don't let *perfection* and *disappointment* rule. Don't let fear of being wrong, making a misstep, or committing a mistake keep you from your destiny.

You have so much more to offer yourself and your community.

Consideration, Conversation, & Collaboration

- How has fear of failure kept you and/or your community from making progress?

- As you and your communities evolve, you can err on the side of *staying safe*, afraid of *what might happen* if you fail. You might even decide not acting will be a more secure route to travel. You know, "Don't send out that CD or newsletter; something bad might happen; you might look foolish!" Brené Brown writes about the power of shame and vulnerability in her book *Daring Greatly*. What is it that creates or stokes the fires of the fear of failure in you and your community? Why do you think the fear takes control of you at times (or often) and keeps you stuck in doing what is *safe?*

- Accepting and learning from mistakes leads to growth. Attempting to avoid ever making a mistake is a foolhardy and growth-limiting endeavor. How can you incorporate this mindset into your community?

- Identify a friend, a colleague, or a community member who, in your eyes, takes risks regularly. Buy him or her a cup of coffee and conduct some question-storming to understand what makes this person tick when it comes to risk taking.

- What other questions do you need to address regarding this topic?

Others, Optimism, & Opportunity[34]

❧

IN 1917, OREGON BEAT PENNSYLVANIA (14-0) in the Rose Bowl. German U-boats stalked international waters. The US Supreme Court upheld the eight-hour workday for railroad workers. The United States officially entered World War I. Babe Ruth played for the Red Sox and pitched Boston to a victory over the New York Yankees.

And, a little girl was born to proud parents in Iowa. She would grow into a woman whose influence, graciousness, and concern for others would leave a meaningful impact around the world. We would come to know this young Iowa girl as Dr. Frances Bartlett Kinne.

My introduction to Dr. Kinne came when I entered Jacksonville (Florida) University as a young college freshman in August of 1971. At the time, she served as the college's Dean of Fine Arts. Little did I know the reach and powerful influence she would have on so many people.

In the fall of 2016, I had the opportunity to catch up with this young-at-heart-and-in-mind centenarian to record a conversation for The Growth and Resilience Network® podcast channel.

Never did I think 45 years earlier that I would be sitting in her den listening and learning, quite literally, at the foot of a master. A master of music, education, and human relationships. And so much more.

Dr. Kinne's life resonates with optimism, grit, and resilience. Her life personified a lesson from her father, "Life is a journey, not a guided tour." We must seize (and many times, make) our opportunities as we move through life. Not just to add to our resume but, rather, to embrace a greater purpose beyond listing the things we accomplish.

During our conversation, she did not want to dwell on her *accomplishments*. Rather, she told me, "My job is to help others. Life is not about me; it's about others."

I thought of how some people may reverse that last sentence and live by "Life is not about others; it's about me!"

You know the folks. Those who remind you at every turn just how great or renowned *they* are. They might even label themselves as your *thought leader.*

For Dr. Kinne, it cannot be about that. It must be about the people in front of her. She treats them as if they are the thought leaders, the pioneers, and the all-stars. She wants to help pave the way for them. Effective teachers intuitively know this. Transformational leaders live it. Dr. Kinne is both.

Thank you, Dr. Kinne.

Consideration, Conversation, & Collaboration

❧

- Who in your community demonstrates that life is about the community, not about them?
- What do you do to demonstrate for people in your community that life is about them, not about you?
- What one new action or process can you and your community members introduce this week to show that your community is not about anyone individual but about the members?
- Listen to the podcast with Dr. Kinne on The Growth and Resilience® podcast channel.[35] Click on Episode #20. What other lessons does Dr. Kinne teach us?
- What other questions do you need to address regarding this topic?

Community Leadership[36]

❧

IF WE FAIL TO PAY attention to the importance of authentic human connections, we do so at our peril. Relationship development is not a soft skill. It is very much an essential skill.

Consider these characteristics that successful and likable leaders tend to possess:[37] approachable, modest, respectful, appreciative, empathetic, and accepting.

A leader—or anyone for that matter—with these characteristics has a human face. She is not a manipulative, power-hungry, and insecure person looking to secure her turf.

People with these characteristics tend to make us feel like we are the only one in the room. As with anyone leading a group, workshop or team, it should never be about the leader. It should always be about the audience—the people in front or behind the leader.

Some may read the above descriptors and say they are too *soft*. A real leader must get results, and that requires tough action and bottom-line thinking. This logic may suggest being *likable* has nothing to do with leadership success.

If a leader has integrity, he knows that performance and quality must be present. His work models what he wants his followers to emulate. He won't get that by constantly barking at and demeaning team members. Oh sure, the demagogic hot head may catch attention—for a while. But soon, he will burn his staff out. They may decide to fly under the radar for fear of being cajoled and embarrassed.

In *The Career Playbook: Essential Advice for Today's Aspiring Young Professional,* James M. Citrin notes that relationship building is a key skill to entering, maintaining, and thriving in a career. You may have heard people talk about "being a fit for a company's culture." According to Citrin, "this means that, if you're interviewing for a job, the interviewer will be assessing you partly based on personal relationships. Do they like you? Do they sense that they can trust you? Do they feel comfortable around you?"[38]

Think about leaders you have followed—and have followed gladly. And think about people you lead. How do you treat them?

Consideration, Conversation, & Collaboration

❧

* Think of a time you worked for a tyrant, or, at the least, a thoroughly disagreeable boss. Perhaps this person disregarded you as a person and treated you as an expendable part in a larger piece of soulless machinery. Each morning when you awakened did you think, "Gee, I can't wait to get back to work for more belittling and distress!"?
* Which of the characteristics of likeable leaders above do your community leaders possess and regularly employ? How do you know? Which need to be developed? What other characteristics exist for likeable leaders?
* Think about leaders you have followed—and have followed gladly. And think about people you lead. How do you treat them?
* What other questions do you need to address regarding this topic?

Important Questions to Ask[39]

❧

ON ONE OF MY SPEAKING engagement trips, I had the opportunity to talk with a person who has been instrumental in training thousands of higher education leaders around our nation.

What did he see as a critical skill for effective leadership? His answer: The ability to listen and then act.

In *Meaningful: The Story of Ideas that Fly,* Bernadette Jiwa reminds us, "We don't change the world by starting with our brilliant idea or dreams. We change the world by helping others to live their dreams." In *Rules for Radicals,* Saul Alinsky states that to communicate we must connect to others' experiences.

Ask questions and then wait for responses. Understand what information you need. Then act. Understand the people in front of you. All require observing and listening. While these skills are often mentioned, they are just as frequently ignored or drowned out by an overwhelming onslaught of information and misinformation. With a world full of noise and look-at-me tweets and posts, how can we fine-tune the needed listening skill?

We must distinguish and separate the noise from the non-noise in the world around us. Shawn Achor provides an insightful rubric[40] for doing just that. Once we understand and apply the criteria for noise, we have a better chance of limiting its debilitating effects on the lives of colleagues, loved ones, and ourselves.

Ask yourself, Achor proposes, if what you attend to or what you endlessly speak about is unusable, untimely, hypothetical, or distracting. More specifically,

- **Unusable**. Will the information you continuously "take in and give out" change your behavior? If not, you are probably wasting time.
    - Example. You follow a news story repeatedly. Since the initial *news alert*, the information remains the same. Nonetheless, you spend hours listening to talking heads give their interpretation. Or you constantly scan your phone for social media updates (other people's agendas). Maybe you spend hours following celebrity stories or the latest intelligence on the NFL draft. And, the information has no impact on your behavior. Nothing changes. Noise?
- **Untimely**. Will you use the information, now? Will it more than likely change in the future when you *might* use it?
    - Example. You get a hurricane alert. It might make landfall in five days. At that point, you have useful information to prepare. However, if you stay glued to the weather channels endlessly for hours, with no new and meaningful information coming in, you need to ask what the benefit is other than getting more worried about something you cannot control and that is still a long way from happening. And, in the case of a weather forecast, it will likely change several times. Noise?
- **Hypothetical**. Do we focus on what *could be* rather than what *is?*
    - Example. I am not picking on the weather prognosticators (really), but do you base plans on the predictions—that may very well be inaccurate. One of my podcast guests[41] has an answer to the meteorological hypothetical. When the forecast calls for 80% rain, he makes a golf tee time. Why?

Because there is 20% for sunshine. Think about economic forecasts. How accurate? How often? Noise?

* **Distracting**. Does the information deter you or stop movement toward your goals?
    * Example. Your goals relate to your career, relationships, health, finances, intellectual development, emotional stability, and spiritual well-being. How much of the onslaught of information you get hit with, and allow yourself to be hit with, relates to those goals? How much gets in the way of goal achievement? Noise?

This week consider where, when, and how you can eliminate noise. Listen to your goals and move in those directions.

Consideration, Conversation, & Collaboration

❦

* What *noise* is distracting your community from its purpose? From where is it coming? What effect does it have upon your community members?
* Who in your community is most susceptible to the noise you identified above?
* What can you do to replace the noise with meaningful input?
* What other questions do you need to address regarding this topic?

A Deeper Dive: VPEER

For this exercise, focus on two communities with which you have membership. One should be a vibrant and prospering community. The other ranks amongst the weakest. Name each one below.

My strongest community is _____.

My weakest community is _____.

Now, for each community answer the questions below.

* **Visualize** the purpose, journey, and membership of your community. What *weak signals* exist to indicate the future of your community will not look like it does now? What does this future focus tell you? What does the community you envision look like? You may wish to initially narrow your focus to one aspect of the community and then broaden your reach after that.
* **Prioritize** the resources you will need, and the actions required to sustain your community and make it thrive into the future. What non-negotiable steps do you need to take? What comes first? How will you identify those **RELATIONSHIPS** that can (or already do) help build and strengthen your community?
* **Exorcise** that which no longer serves or nourishes your community. How can you minimize or eliminate the pernicious effects of certain relationships? Where does this fit with your prioritization of resources and actions? Who will help you identify these factors? Where will this fit in your prioritization? Who can help you?
* **Exercise** and strengthen the emotional, physical, and spiritual dimensions of life. Community building can be challenging

work. How will you and your members build and maintain a healthy lifestyle moving forward? Where can you find this on your list of priorities?

* **Realize** your visualization. How often will you stop to evaluate your progress? How will you realize if you are faithfully following the four steps above (visualize, prioritize, exorcise, and exercise)?

Relevance

Having a connection to the issue at hand.

❦

RELATED TERMS INCLUDE: AUTHENTICITY, CORE values, critical thinking, distractions, fitness, goals, present moment, relationships, and *resources.*[42]

A TRANSFORMATIONAL STORY ABOUT COMMUNITY: "TRUST AS A CORE VALUE"

A few decades after the Civil War, Clara White, a former slave, saw a need and acted. Some of her Jacksonville, Florida, neighbors did not have enough to eat. With scarce resources, she fed what she could to whom she could. A mission took hold.

In the 1930s, at the beginning of the Great Depression, Clara's daughter, Eartha, saw greater privation, and she acted by expanding the mission from a *soup kitchen* to a community development center meeting needs for food, shelter, and support services.

Today the Clara White Mission[43] feeds, houses, educates, and ministers to the physical, emotional, and spiritual needs of the homeless and low-income. Regardless of the service provided, the goal is to provide relevant training and support for long-term self-sufficiency.

CEO and President of the Clara White Mission, Ms. Ju' Coby Pittman,[44] understands that each client arrives at the front door "broken, with a laundry bag of challenges," and in need of someone to believe in and assist them. They require a community of resources.

But how does an agency ministering to the needs of a transient population develop a sense of community? Is that even possible? Pittman told me it is possible, and it comes down to one core value. Trust.

Trust does not come from words in a mission statement. It grows from authentic relationships and having relevant conversations about people's rainbows—their dreams. Often, clients do not believe the Clara White Mission can do what it says it can.

"How does someone care this much about me?" they wonder.

Recognizing that everyone's situation is different, the Clara White Mission support system of counselors, teachers, and administrators connects with each client as an individual, a person. They listen. And they share the possibilities for a brighter future.

Once enrolled in the program and with basic survival needs met, the clients begin to see the relevance of the Clara White Mission services to their lives. Clients can enroll in training and certification programs such as culinary arts and forklift operation as well as construction and site safety. They also have access to a program that provides agricultural education for food desert residents.

Rather than passive observers, the clients remain actively involved in their journey. The staff share the mission and history of the center with clients. They hear *alumni* of the mission's programs recount their respective journeys. And those stories resonate with the lives of the new clients. They feel heard and engaged in the process. Pittman shared that the mission provides "a hand up, not a hand out." Respect and trust build as a result.

The clients enter into a partnership with the mission and they, in turn, help new clients see the relevance in what the Clara White Mission does each day for each client. They give back to the community.

"It's not a job; it's a ministry," states Pittman. "Everyone has a story, and our job is to listen. What we think might be best for them, might *not* be the best for them."

Mark Twain reportedly said that the two most important days of our lives are the day we are born and the day we discover why we were born.

Pittman said she finds her *why,* the relevance for what she does, in the motto of Clara and Ertha White:

> *Do all the good you can,*
> *In all the ways you can,*
> *For all the people you can,*
> *And all the places you can,*
> *While you can.*

That is relevant. That forms trust. And it builds community.

Before You Start

❧

As the story of The Clara White Mission (above) shares, "everyone has a story and it's our job to listen." In what ways does your community *listen* to the *stories* of its members—and then appreciate and act on those stories?

Consider communities—vibrant as well as those that struggle—to which you belong. How can the concept of **RELEVANCE** help the vibrant ones prosper and the struggling ones grow?

Think of a dynamic community to which you belong. In what ways does understanding **RELEVANCE** contribute to its growth and resilience? Conversely, what do your struggling communities lack when it comes to **RELEVANCE**?

Below you will find blog post excerpts related to the concept of **RELEVANCE**. Choose one, read it, and consider its message. You will probably note that one or more of the other Seven Rs come into play as well. These core values mutually reinforce one another. Begin a conversation about how you and your community do use and can use the thoughts to foster and sustain community.

Then, repeat with the other blog excerpts.

After each excerpt, you will find several suggestions and specific questions on how to bring the teachings of the piece to life in your community. Rather than settling for general answers, use the following three-step model to help you be more actionable with your responses.

1. Establish a realistic, feasible, time-bound plan for implementing your proposed actions.
2. Execute your plan. Make sure all involved understand their roles and responsibilities.
3. Evaluate your progress on a regular basis. Adjust course as needed.

We are all Related[45]

CHIEF SEATTLE IS CREDITED WITH saying, "We are the web of life; whatever we do to the web we do to ourselves."

The Japanese concept of *genba* means that to understand something we have go to the place where the work is done. For me, a visit to Standing Rock Reservation in North Dakota was like that. It reminded me that we are all truly part of the web of life.

Mitakuye Oyasin. The Lakota phrase literally means "Whoever are all my relatives." On my visit to Sitting Bull College in Ft. Yates, North Dakota, in 2013, I was struck by the many references to our connections with the universe.

I had dinner with one of Sitting Bull's great-great-great grandsons, Ron His Horse is Thunder. Ron and his wife live in a comfortable prairie house on the Missouri River. Horses, cows, deer, and pheasant surround them. And snakes do as well. Ron shared the following story.

He found a rather large rattlesnake in his driveway. Rather than kill it, he picked it up with a pitch fork and toted it a distance from the house. He placed it on the ground and then spoke to the snake. He simply told him that he was free to go—and not return. Ron recognized the snake's existence; he wished the snake to do the same. He then sprinkled tobacco around the edges of his property. Four years later, no rattlesnakes have returned.

During my visit I had the opportunity to spend some time with Reuben FastHorse[46]. He reminded me that "we all interact in some kind of way." What one does for or to another has relevance for that person and the community.

Mitakuye Oyasin.

Consideration, Conversation, & Collaboration

❦

* React to "we all interact in some kind of way." How does this relate to your neighborhood? Your workplace? In what ways can your community capitalize on this sentiment?
* What issues resonate in your neighborhood? What *hot button* topics bring people to meetings, for instance? Why do you believe these issues resonate?
* If you had to advise a community on how to attack apathy, what would be your top three suggestions?
* At times we can *understand* an issue. We know the details and the processes. At the same time, however, we may not *understand* how the issue connects emotionally with people. And, we may miss how the same issue can stir up far different feelings in different neighbors. How do you go beyond mere understanding to emotional connection? How can you make it personal in a good way? What do you do to remain relevant within your community and how does your community remain relevant to its members?[47]
* What other questions do you need to address regarding this topic?

Drive Like Your Kids Live Here[48]

❦

I OFTEN ENCOURAGE AUDIENCES TO consider their job performance from the perspective of whom they serve. If I am speaking to teachers, I want them to think about the impact their teaching has on their students. I encourage corporate audiences to envision the service or product they provide for their customers. And while this image of service delivery can help get a conversation started about effective relationships, it lacks a certain urgency. It can end up being a rather academic exercise of *us* providing for *them*. Disembodied. Devoid of emotional connection.

To get a bit more *buy-in* to the exercise, I have asked faculty to consider their children (or partner, or grandmother, or some other person close to them) sitting in their classrooms and in the classes of their colleagues. Once they have that image, I ask them about job performance. Are they satisfied with the level of competence, energy, and passion that their loved one receives in that setting?

It's the same question but with a tad more relevance.

Some neighborhoods post the sign, "Drive Like Your Kids Live Here." That makes an emotional connection. It has a better chance of being relevant to the drivers (the *audience*) passing by. For parents, they can see the faces of their own offspring.

That sign reminds me that when we attempt to connect with people, we need to be relevant to them. We need to know their story and connect to that story. Think of politicians with large followings. They establish an emotional association with the people in front of them. Some use that for good and some for ill. But all make the message meaningful to their consumers.

An article I wrote about effective faculty development[49] proposed questions to consider when creating growth opportunities. Below, I have modified a few of those questions to reflect beyond teachers to the broader *community*.

1. How can we connect community development activities with individual career and personal trajectories? How can we help members explore the various spokes of professional growth?
2. How can we, as much as possible, let community members have a choice/control over their personal and/or professional development? How can we let them identify their needs and passions, and then consider what programming will meet those self-identified needs and passions?
3. What does the community culture do to promote and support true opportunities for ongoing renewal, recovery, and self-care for its leadership?
4. How can we allow and encourage members to share their personal passions with other community members?
5. How can we encourage opportunities for examining and discussing what works, what does not work, and what may work in the community?
6. How can we find ways to incorporate laughter and creativity into community development?
7. How can we support and encourage members to attend and participate at national, regional, and local conferences and workshops that address our community needs?
8. How can we develop local *home-grown* opportunities for growth opportunities?

Keep the conversation practical, purposeful, and personal.

Consideration, Conversation, & Collaboration

❧

- What are the relevant issues for your community's sustainability? How do you know?
- Are all members of your community made to feel as if they are relevant? How do you know?
- What opportunities exist within your community for members to share their expertise and passions? What opportunities need to be created?
- How can you connect the descriptors of *inclusive* and *like-minded* to the concept of **RELEVANCE** in your community?
- What other questions do you need to address regarding this topic?

Remain Relevant[50]

◈

RELEVANCE GOES BEYOND MESSAGE. WHILE content and methodology affect connections, so does the person or group who delivers the message.

Once you understand the issues that resonate with your community, you need to pause and ask, "Am I relevant to this community? Do I bring something of value to the conversation?"

Prior to working with any audience, I invest several hours in emails and phone conferences with the contracting institution or organization. I ask a lot of questions about their expectations and needs. Having sat through my fair share of irrelevant speakers and inconsequential programs, I make it my responsibility to understand what my audience needs. To be relevant to my audiences I must be meaningful to the people in front of me. My appearance must be about them[51] not about me. That means tailoring the message to their situation as best I can.

In her book *Meaningful: The Story of Ideas that Fly*, Bernadette Jiwa drives home one main point: "Start the innovation journey with the customer's story and allow our customers to become not just our target, but our muse."[52]

Whoever sits in our *audiences* we would do well to consider Jiwa's advice. What is the purpose of our talk or service or product or meeting? Is it to be relevant to us or the people we serve? If it is not relevant to them, are we serving them? Why should the community care about what you say or who you are?

The first day of the semester, I started with my students' dreams and lives and went from there. The approach to the course material had to resonate with and connect to the people in front of me. I had to attempt to understand their story rather than force feed my story. I needed to tap into their feelings and emotions. To them, college was not simply about a degree. It was about a better life for them and their families.

Do we take time to experience, or at least attempt to understand, our community members' experiences?

Jiwa's book reinforced for me that success is not what we make but, rather, the difference we make with our product or our service in people's lives. She challenges us to consider, "Before you/your product/your service came on the scene, what did people do? After you/your product/ your service came on the scene, what did people do? The trap we fall into is trying to tell people how life-changing our widget is. If it changes their lives, we won't have to tell them."

Relevance. Meaning. Connection.

Consideration, Conversation, & Collaboration

❧

* How do you remain relevant for your community?
* Examine a service or product your community provides. How do you know members want or need it? Do the same for a new service, product, or feature that has been considered for the community?
* When you consider the future needs of your community, what weak signals do you see that tell you what is relevant today might be irrelevant next week, month, year, or decade?
* Consider a service or product in which your community invests a significant amount of resources. In what way has this enhanced your community? How do you know?
* What other questions do you need to address regarding this topic?

Core Values[53]

❦

WHEN IT COMES TO COMMUNITY, what guides your actions?

I am constantly seeking input and *game film* to help me with my movement toward improvement. I meet with trusted mentors and advisors to chart professional activities. Among other agenda items, we discussed how to connect core values to articulated goals.

Before I could list my goals going forward, I had to identify what I held dear and important. Without a clear awareness of that, how could I chart goals and direction for the future? The values provide the WHYs for my WHATs (goals).

We all need to be aware of what guides our actions. Is it the chase for financial wealth, ego gratification, and security? Meaningful relationships? Intimacy? Health? Significance? Legacy?

While we need to have clear boundaries and limits in our professional and personal lives, it is clear they are inextricably connected. One constantly affects the other.

Do your core values reflect that connection?

Consideration, Conversation, & Collaboration

❧

- Set aside some time this week to write your top five core values. Something about seeing them in print makes them real. The process leads to self-examination about how true you have been to these values.
- When you look at these core values, where do your actions align and where do they not?
- Select one of your communities. List the top five core values of that community. What does this community do that reflects its stated core values?
- In what ways do your individual core values align or not align with the community core values? Relate this to your earlier discussion about what community means to you.
- Compare your list of community core values with a fellow community member. Discuss any insights you gain.
- What other questions do you need to address regarding this topic?

Change: Comprehension & Communication[54]

❦

How do you define *learning*? What causes and influences learning? How much of your schooling exposed you to a stream of fire-hosed arcane knowledge with little connection and relevance to your life? Do you consider that to be *learning*?

One measure to consider is whether our thinking or behaviors have changed in a sustainable manner. *Learning* isolated facts that are promptly lost after the test is not learning. That's memorization. Or as one teacher so aptly noted, such an exchange is nothing less than "bulimic education."[55] Take it in, then spit it out. A tumble of facts in and a tumble of facts out. Relevance is lost in the exchange.

Even engaging in a well-articulated conversation or debate has questionable learning value if there is no change in one's mental mindset.

In 2015, I had the honor of being placed in the spotlight at the Atlantic Beach [Florida] Songwriters' Night. I was humbled to get the invitation, and once I was sitting on stage that feeling magnified. I didn't have stage fright. I felt appreciation for others. From my vantage point that evening, I was able to see accomplished songwriters in the audience. As I told them, "I am honored, but I am not a songwriter. I do write songs, but that does not make me a songwriter. I play guitar. That does not make me a guitar player."

Just because I have lifted weights for years does not make me a trainer, either.

Someone who writes is not necessarily a writer. The inimitable Truman Capote reportedly said, "That isn't writing; that's typing."

Whether we teach a classroom full of eager and not so-eager students, orient new students to the university, train staff in our organization, teach a young girl to play guitar, or discuss a community issue, we look for some level of change. Some type of movement toward improvement.

Calling it *teaching* does not mean the audience experienced learning. Just because it was tossed, doesn't mean it was caught. Just because it was talked, doesn't mean it was taught.

The spin on Capote's wisdom for me would be, "That's not teaching; that's talking."

How do you connect with your community members? If they and you leave meetings with the exact same mental model—no adjustments—then can we say anything was *learned*? Nothing has changed, and there is no sustainable difference.

Why are we so enamored with filling people's minds with long lists of stuff that, by themselves, do not help them? Why not help the person form meaningful and useful patterns that either relate to or build upon their experiences?

Think of your workplace and the last staff, board, or stockholder meeting. How relevant was the presented material? Beyond the facts, charts, and numbers that reflected the health and growth of the organization, was there a connection to the people in the room? Did the speakers drone on and on—or did someone decide to break the script, and make the message memorable and actionable?[56]

What are the implications of focusing on patterns, structures, and trends for your workplace? Do you want your team members to remember isolated facts or would you rather they connect those facts in a meaningful pattern, so they can be successful for your organization and the people it serves?

The same for your community meeting examining parks, safe sidewalks to school, and family-oriented recreational zones. Do people need a recitation of statistics? Not likely.

Do you want to teach facts or people?

Consideration, Conversation, & Collaboration

◈

- What emerging patterns or structures do you see for the future of your community? Pick one. What do people need to know about this coming trend? Why? How will you convey this needed information?
- The brief video "Structures for Organization (A Teaching and Learning Model)"[57] provides a few proactive questions that may help get your community conversation started about structures of *community* organization.
- Confer with a neighbor about the above video on structures. In what ways can you connect this to your community or neighborhood association?
- What kind of training and coaching program do you have for your community leaders? Lead a conversation regarding how an effective mentoring program[58] can connect with what your community or team needs to address.
- What other questions do you need to address regarding this topic?

Hell, Yeah![59]

❧

DURING ONE OF MY PODCAST recordings, film producer Pepper Lindsey[60] posed an intriguing question: "What does success look like to you?"

Consider it for yourself. Is success for you measured by money, fame, a certain title, ego, an opulent lifestyle, a simple lifestyle, making a difference in your community, driving a larger car, or taking trips? Something else?

Derek Sivers, in his book *Anything You Want: 40 Lessons for a New Kind of Entrepreneur,*[61] asks a similarly interesting question: "How do you grade yourself?"

Does success depend on whether people notice you or if you have your name on a park or building? Or is it connected to the programs you helped start in that park or building—programs that will live well beyond you and your name recognition? These questions tie directly to why we want to do what we want to do.

Goals can be powerful motivators. They provide direction, purpose, energy, and relevance for our lives. And, if we are not clear on the WHAT and the WHY of our goals they can lead us in unhealthy directions. We may even beat ourselves up because we have not achieved a certain goal ("Life is passing me by." "I'm not getting any younger!").

How do we grade ourselves? How do we define success?

Be aware of and understand the assumptions you make when establishing your goals—and ask whether they meet your definition of success.

Do you have "Hell, Yeah Goals!" Or "Hell, No Goals!"? Do you even care about goals or do you meander from day to day?

Do a *Second READ* when determining whether to accept or reject a professional engagement or a community-based commitment.

* **Relationship.** Will you work with people you enjoy and respect? Will you grow because of your interaction? Will they have the opportunity to grow because of you? This requires validation by and for all parties and not manipulation by any party.
* **Enthusiasm**. Will you enjoy preparing for and doing the event? What will sustain your energy and excitement through project completion?
* **Authenticity**. Will the project allow you to be your true self? Does the task resonate with you as a person? Is this important to you? Or will you need to deny who you are for the sake of the project? How does this make you feel?
* **Difference**. Will your participation make a difference in the lives of the people connected to the project—and beyond?

Finally, ask yourself if your goal is to be involved in *any* project or activity, or does it need to be the *right* project or activity?

Consideration, Conversation, & Collaboration

❦

- Apply the *Second READ* to your community. Pick one issue that confronts the community. How do questions of relationship, enthusiasm, authenticity, and difference connect to the issue? Where is the community strong? Where can it become stronger? Who can help?

- Consider what your community does or needs to do to *make a difference* in the lives of its members. What stands out—what separates your community from others?

- Confer with your community members. Have everyone list five *Hell, Yeah* goals for the community. Compare your lists. What do you believe your next step should be?

- What other questions do you need to address regarding this topic?

Question Assumptions[62]

❦

WHAT STRATEGIES CAN HELP US become more aware of what and why we do what we do?

Once we understand what we do, we then need to examine why we do what we do. Our assumptions not only invite us to ask questions, they beg for questions. Can we separate fact from fiction, rationale from rationalization?

Consider a baseball player with a .300 batting average. Experts consider that an excellent season. But if you look at that in another way, those productive batters have failed more than two thirds of the time they are at the plate. What's going on here?

These star players understand that they must confront what challenges them in the batter's box. To stay in *the show,* they need to get beyond their hitting limits. They practice; they watch game film. They keep going and growing. They have reflected, responded, and created movement to improvement. They challenge themselves with each pitch. They assume they will master the next pitch.

Successful athletes follow what the Japanese call *kaizen.* Literally, change is good. They make constant little adjustments to improve what they do. The process is not just for what is not working, but it also can help us examine what does work—and understand how it can work better. And so it is with each of us as well. We all have our limits—and beliefs about those limits.

When we end up settling for something less than what we can achieve, we limit ourselves. Rather than confront our assumptions about what is in front of us or what we are about to face, we will rationalize why where we are is *good enough.*

Or we might run and numb by drinking alcohol, taking drugs, staying at the office longer than we need to, exercising excessively, or wasting inordinate amounts of time on social media or in front of the TV. The temporary numbing avoids confronting the crisis. After you numb, the crisis is still present, maybe worse. Are you happy with that picture?

The limits remain, and they limit our potentiality.

In short, challenge your assumptions and create action—movement toward improvement. One little step at a time. Kaizen!

Consideration, Conversation, & Collaboration

❧

* What does your community need to focus on to experience *movement to improvement*? What has it been avoiding? What does it need to confront head on—and the sooner the better?
* Is kaizen one of your community's core values? How can you incorporate it?
* Where in your life, this week, can you practice kaizen? What assumptions do you need to begin or continue working to understand? Where would you benefit by making little tweaks that will make you a better version of yourself?
* Where can your community benefit from kaizen?

A Deeper Dive: VPEER

❧

For this exercise, focus on two communities in which you have membership. One should be a vibrant and prospering community. The other ranks amongst the weakest.

My strongest community is _____.

My weakest community is _____.

Now, for each community answer the questions below.

- **Visualize** the purpose, journey, and membership of your community. What *weak signals* exist to indicate the future of your community will not look like the past? What does this future focus tell you? What does the community you envision look like?
- **Prioritize** the resources you will need, and the actions required to sustain your community—and make it thrive into the future. What non-negotiable steps do you need to take? What comes first? How will you distinguish between **RELEVANT** and irrelevant resources to help build and strengthen your community?
- **Exorcise** that which no longer serves or nourishes your community. How can you minimize or eliminate the pernicious effects? Where does this fit with your prioritization of resources and actions? Who will help you identify these factors? Where will this fit in your prioritization? What is no longer relevant?
- **Exercise** contributes to the various dimensions of an individual's and community's health. Community building can be challenging work. What relevant programs exist to assist you and your members to maintain your emotional, physical, and spiritual health moving forward? Are these programs on your

list of priorities? What programs or resources need to be added and what needs to be eliminated?

* **Realize** your visualization. How often will you stop to evaluate your progress? How will you realize if you are faithfully following the four steps above (visualize, prioritize, exorcise, and exercise)?

Resources

Sources of support to connect and help one grow, recover, prosper, and lend a hand.

⋘⋙

RELATED TERMS INCLUDE: COLLABORATION, COMMUNICATION, *goals, gratitude, leadership, mentorship, relationships, and technology.*[63]

A TRANSFORMATIONAL STORY ABOUT COMMUNITY: "IT'S EASY TO BE LEFT BEHIND"[64]

In the mid-1990s, the Walt Disney Company brought the principles of new urbanism to life when it broke ground on Celebration, Florida. Located minutes from Disney's Orlando theme parks, Celebration was planned to be a "complete diverse, walkable, compact, and vibrant place to live, learn, work, and play. This created community would be a traditional American town built anew."[65]

While visitors may focus on the architecture, mixed use zoning, mansions, townhomes, greenspace, cozy shops and bistros, Celebration is more than bricks, mortar, and homeowner association covenants. Look deeper—just like in any vibrant community—and we are reminded that people live in those houses, traverse the streets, and patronize the shops. Old and young need more than quaint streets and manufactured snowflakes during the holiday season. They want a sense of belonging and meaning.

Enter the Celebration Foundation, a curator of resources for the community. Its board members recognized early on that their best resources were the residents of the community. The key was to tap into those people, the community's biggest asset. The Foundation knew that without people, there is no community.

When the Foundation came to life in 1996, it brought together the community gatekeepers who helped identify and assess needs of the greater community. Over the years, it has reached out to the homeless in need of a meal, to young girls searching for positive role models, and to high school students looking for post-secondary direction.

In 2015, the Foundation launched *Thriving In Place*, a resource program for the *mature* Celebration population. Born from conversations with Celebration residents, it became clear that neighbors aged 55 and older were facing challenging situations to remain in their homes. Some needed assistance with basic home maintenance, while others required transportation to and from doctors, hospitals, the grocery store, special events, or places of worship. A few had to confront the difficult situation to give up their homes and independent lifestyle. You could say these older residents (and some with disabilities) had trouble "aging in place." Foundation board member Eileen Crawford, however, saw this from another perspective.

She said that "aging in place" may describe what the residents were doing, but not who they wanted to be. They did not want merely to survive. They may have been aging individuals, but they most definitely were not decrepit people waiting to be warehoused. They wanted to thrive.

Executive Director Gloria Niec credits the organic growth of *Thriving In Place* to a methodical process. As a skilled facilitator and leader, she knew you do not develop a resource without meaningful input from, and deep conversation with, those who would use that resource.

It took two years to gather the research needed to understand what the program had to provide, what the program needed to look like, who would participate, and how it would be supported and funded. Not a minor undertaking.

Today, its mission states:

Thriving In Place is a community-based membership program designed to help residents stay in their home and the community they love. If you are at least 55 years old or a person with a disability of any age, you are eligible to become a member of our program. It enables residents to live in their own homes leading healthy, safe, independent and productive lives.

Starting with a pioneer group of 20, membership more than quintupled by 2018. What do members get for their yearly membership of $1/day (or $520/year for a couple)? At one of their weekly Friday luncheons, the assembled program members provided unscripted testimony about the impact of the program. For them, *Thriving In Place:*

* Establishes community—caring for one another;
* Relieves loneliness;
* Builds friendships;
* Includes opportunities for the disabled;
* Offers the ability to volunteer—to give back to their community;
* Provides transportation to events or to and from medical appointments; and
* Creates stay-in-touch phone calling, which, in turn, provides assurances to long-distance family members that their elderly parents are doing well.

One member stood and shared that the program is a reminder to "be kind and loving to everyone you meet. Because, everyone is fighting a battle."

Another poignantly stated, "We are slowing down, as people around us are moving faster. It's easy to be left behind." *Thriving In Place* provides access to resources, so they will not be left behind.

Social capital helps create a full life. Research tells us if we can move beyond weak social ties to more meaningful and authentic connections, our chances for longer life expand.[66]

And, according to program manager Mary Pat Rosenthal, socialization continues to be the common denominator—the glue—for the *Thriving In Place* members. The activities, events, excursions, and the intergenerational volunteer opportunities allow the members to be involved, active, and contributing community resources themselves. They still have talents and gifts to grow and to share.[67] Remember, as board member Crawford first stated, these folks are doing anything but "aging in place!"

When we speak of resources, *things* and *services* may come to mind. Do not, however, forget the relationships. Relationships remain the secret sauce. Without them what do we have? Connected people create, nurture, and sustain the best resource a community has to offer.

Thriving In Place proves a home is more than the sum of its architectural codes, zoning requirements, and pedestrian friendly streets. Home is a feeling of comfort, peace, and community.

When I asked Rosenthal, the program manager, what kept her coming back to the program each day she smiled and said, "It's about the people."

Resources take on many forms. Beyond material things, healthy relationships offer a powerful foundation that, really, supports all others.

Before You Start

IN WHAT WAYS DOES YOUR community build social capital to help its members not be left behind?

Consider communities—vibrant ones as well as those that struggle—to which you belong. How do **RESOURCES** help the vibrant groups prosper and the struggling ones grow? List the top three **RESOURCES** that help your vibrant communities grow and be well. What **RESOURCES** do your struggling communities need to focus on moving forward?

For instance, think of a dynamic community to which you belong. In what ways do the **RESOURCES** in that community contribute to its growth and resilience? Conversely, what do your struggling communities lack when it comes to **RESOURCES**?

Below you will find blog post excerpts related to the concept of **RESOURCES**. Choose one, read it, and consider its message. You will probably note that one or more of the other Seven Rs come into play as well. These core values mutually reinforce one another. Begin a conversation about how you and your community can use the points to foster and sustain community.

Then, repeat with the other blog excerpts.

After each excerpt, you will find several suggestions and specific questions on how to bring the teachings of the piece to life in your community. Rather than settling for general answers, use the following three-step model to help you be more actionable with your responses.

1. Establish a realistic, feasible, time-bound plan for implementing your proposed actions.
2. Execute your plan. Make sure all involved understand their roles and responsibilities.
3. Evaluate your progress on a regular basis. Adjust course as needed.

Collisions & Serendipity[68]

⤐⤏

COLLISIONS REPRESENT OPPORTUNITIES. VISIONARY TONY Hsieh believes we need to "maximize collisions to accelerate serendipity."[69] That is, we need to put ourselves in the position to connect with as many pertinent resources as possible to increase chances for progress, growth, learning, and connections. Unthinking isolation can create stagnation.

As a teacher, I loved going into the classroom each day, closing the door, and working with my students. The autonomy represented a benefit of teaching. It also had a potentially devastating drawback. If I (and my colleagues) did not stay vigilant, we lost opportunities to maximize collisions. We could become insular. Chances for serendipity (growth) decreased.

The same holds true in corporate and neighborhood settings. If managers across the company landscape remain insular, they can end up repeating redundant routines and retreating behind territorial barriers. Whether you work in the corporate space, higher education, healthcare, or community activism, consider how you break down silos and build bridges.

At my former college, I was fortunate to have the opportunity (along with a colleague who was a counselor with student services) to develop and deliver a workshop series that looked at student challenges. We brought faculty and advisors together to share counseling insights and teaching strategies. We connected with one another.

I find it interesting that so many people willingly share intimate experiences and tribulations with their *friends* on social media, but will not walk across the hall to seek feedback from colleagues sharing the same workspace challenges.

Reflect on your neighborhood. Do people congregate on the front porches or in their fenced backyards? Do they leave for work each day from the garage only to return to the same garage, closing the door, and exiting the car directly into the house? Where do you find or create opportunities for collisions?

Collisions create opportunities for collaboration and communication. There is no need to be an island.

Consideration, Conversation, & Collaboration

❧

- Look at your workplace or community-based activities. Consider all the great resources you have. How do you discover them? How do you share them?
- How do you create and maximize *collisions* so that others know what you do, what you need, and what you can offer?
- How do the members of your community come to know about the resources available for them to grow?
- What other questions do you need to address regarding this topic?

Come Together: Food, Friends, and Family[70]

༼ §৶

THE SEVEN RS OVERLAP. ONE does not exist without one or more of the others. Relationships cannot be overestimated as a potent resource for community development. Whether sharing dinner at a neighbor's home or eating in the communal lunch room at work, relationships strengthen resources.

Consider the word *hygge* or coziness that comes to us from the Danes. It describes the feeling associated when "you tuck in around a candlelit table with good drinks, good friends, and conversation" says Dan Buettner.[71] Conjure up the vision, if you will, of a warm candlelit room with civil and convivial interactions.

One study[72] examined "the association between eating together and team performance." The researchers investigated "field research within firehouses in a large city." They found "eating and talking intertwined as long as the neighboring eaters are familiar with each other."

I arrived at the same findings more than sixty years ago sitting around the table in my Aunt Philomena's kitchen. Maybe not the same research rigor—but similar findings. And better meatballs, I'm sure!

Another study[73] found a "50% increased likelihood of survival for participants with stronger social relationships." In other words, according to these findings, if we can move beyond weak social ties to more meaningful and authentic connections, our chances for longer life expand.

Harvard has been tracking[74] adult male development since 1938 and has found that "good relationships keep us happier and healthier."

When I look back at my Aunt Philomena's weekly gatherings I do not remember much about the food. Sure, I remember it was delicious, plentiful, homemade, and spicy. But I would be hard pressed to name a specific dish or to say her meatballs or lasagna were better than my mother's.

What I remember (in pretty good detail) about those meals focuses on conversation (often loud and emotional exchanges), bocce in the backyard, and laughter. The food might have brought us together; the bonding kept us coming back.

Consideration, Conversation, & Collaboration

❦

* What kind of events or gatherings does your community organize around food?
* When you gather for *food events,* who organizes and where do they occur?
* What do you consider the top three resources your community has to offer its members?
* How do your community leaders promote and share these resources? How do you take advantage of them?
* As you look to the future, what one resource do you need to develop for community sustainability? How do you know? When will you start?
* What other questions do you need to address regarding this topic?

Ask Questions[75]

⟨✦⟩

CONSIDER THE COMMON THREAD IN following:

- In early 2016, I traveled to Gainesville, Florida to record a podcast about Prader-Willi Syndrome[76]. Early in the conversation, the executive director said that one of the important things The Arc of Alachua County does is to "listen and ask questions. You have to really know what someone wants out of life before you work toward that...."

- The title of a keynote presentation I delivered to a group of facility managers who daily have to address difficult situations with internal and external customers was "What Important Questions Should I Be Asking—And How Do I Know They Are the Correct Questions?"

- Marilee Adams's book *Change Your Questions, Change Your Life*[77] uses a parable to help us focus on the choices we all have when confronted with a confounding situation. Do we move along the Learner Mindset Path asking questions of ourselves, or do we follow the Judger Mindset Path that casts blame on others? One leads to growth, the other to a muddled pit.

Too often we may find ourselves, colleagues, supervisors, friends, neighbors, or family members in the Judger role, quickly making assumptions about this or that and then smugly telling someone else what they should or should not do.[78]

The listening skill typically goes AWOL. It seems that people will weigh in on most anything—whether they know about it or not; whether we ask them to or not. Rather than say "Can you tell me more?" or "Why do you think this or that is so?" they will opine. And God forbid if they were to utter, "I don't know about that. Can you educate me?"

Help yourself and others learn and grow. It really is OK not to know all the answers.

Consideration, Conversation, & Collaboration

❦

* This week, how can you more effectively listen to the person in front of you and ask questions? When and where will you begin?
* Consider a challenge your community faces at this moment. Rather than brainstorm, hold a question-storming session with a community group. What are the top ten questions you may want to consider before you start attempting solutions?
* After you have developed the ten questions in the step above, develop a list of resources that could address those challenges. Which do you have? Which do you need? Which do you have and need to tweak to make more effective?
* What other questions do you need to address regarding this topic?

On Collegiality and Caring[79]

❦

DURING MY UNDERGRADUATE YEARS AT Jacksonville University (Florida), I spent a fair number of hours in the campus library. On the second floor, students found study rooms where they could isolate themselves for quiet time. I recall some of these rooms having a typewriter for those needing to hammer out a term paper.

When I taught at Florida State College at Jacksonville, the library had quiet rooms for students to study or practice for presentations. (No typewriters to be found, though!) These study groups helped students understand concepts, share ideas, review notes, and encourage one another during exam preparation. Collaborative growth and development.

The image of students pulling all-nighters notwithstanding, some campuses now provide nap zones and nap stations.[80] A rested student is a better-prepared student, the thinking goes.

When I visited the Zappos headquarters in April of 2017, I met *Zappos Mayor,* Tony Ferrara. In follow-up emails, I asked the *Mayor* about the Zappos nap room. Were there any metrics on its use and success? He said,

Yes, we do have a nap room here at Zappos for those folks that may need a little power nap during their break or lunch times.

In addition to the nap room, we have several miscellaneous benefits here at Zappos....We don't provide these extras specifically for the purpose of quantifying their results. We provide them as part of building and maintaining culture through employee engagement. For example, we don't monitor who uses the nap rooms at all. They're there for the benefit and convenience of team members, not for analyzing metrics.[81]

More than likely, your workplace does not have a nap room. The culture and the leadership may not support such a departure from the industrial work model. What can and do you do to promote well-being?

Start with a group of community members you trust; people who understand or want to understand the experiences of the community and its members. You can function as a collegial support group as you talk and share ideas. You might find that you need to engage a facilitator at some point to bring your *movement* to a higher level.

At times, just having community members acknowledge that they hear our concerns, and maybe share those concerns, provides the shot of energy we need. Great start. But what action will you take beyond the words? What will your collective resiliency plan look like? When will you start to consider, converse, and collaborate? How will you create a safe place to grow?

Consideration, Conversation, & Collaboration

❦

* Rather than waiting for or blaming *them* to do something, get creative and start a movement yourself. Consider your own *resource group*. Create a critical mass for a *resilience movement*. It could start over a cup of coffee or a walk around the campus during lunch. Who needs to be in your critical mass?

* Focus on positives. What workplace or neighborhood resources create avenues for growth and how can you create more of these? What resources do you have access to now, and which do you need access to in the future?

* What resources does your community use to recharge itself? Block parties? Neighborhood dinners? Running errands for one another? Walking clubs?

* What other questions do you need to address regarding this topic?

Take Care of Your Greatest Resource[82]

⌁

WITH EVERY DECEMBER INVARIABLY COME thoughts of New Year's Resolutions. Just as inevitably, the undeniable breaking of those resolutions will occur within the first few weeks of the New Year. Many of us start with the desire to be in good shape, better shape, or best shape. But something happens on the way to that better version of ourselves. Many will give up. Two of the perennially broken resolutions are to lose weight and get fit.

The reasons vary from unrealistic expectations (we overwhelm ourselves) to lack of action (we underwhelm ourselves). Call it "Big Intentions—Minimal Action."[83] If you lack discipline and the work ethic to make your dreams come true, the dearth of action will create its own reality.

There are several strategies that we can all use to help us identify our goals, act, and enjoy the reality we want to create.

If physical fitness is part of life fitness, why do many of us "fall off the fitness wagon"? I explored this during Episode #9[84] on *The Growth and Resilience Network*® podcast channel. Personal trainer and competitive power lifter Charles Bailey provided insights from nearly 30 years working with people on their life fitness goals. He reminded us that we all live multi-dimensional lives and for that reason it's difficult to consider *physical* conditioning without also considering other dimensions such as the emotional, social, and occupational components of our lives. And that requires awareness and discipline.

But how many of us stop and think about these fitness components? As Charles said during the recording session, "How do you walk around in something you were born with and not know anything about it or not be aware of what affects it?"

What resources can help you be more aware of and take care of your body? Start with your own goals and then find support. For instance,

* Don't overwhelm yourself. Be realistic with your goals and timing. Know why you want those goals. If you have started a fitness program in the past, and then fell off the wagon, do you know why that occurred? How can your goals, this time, remain sustainable?
* If you use a trainer, *audition* him or her before engaging that person for your fitness regimen. In the podcast noted above, Charles suggested a few key characteristics and qualities to look for in a trainer.
* A trainer needs to pay attention to the client—and the client needs to pay attention to the trainer. Do you know what to look for during the first session and beyond?
* Know your current fitness level and where you want to go. Consult your doctor/healthcare professional as needed to make sure you embark on and stay on a healthy and safe fitness program. Take in as much accurate and appropriate information as you can. Do you have an awareness about your current fitness; understand the assumptions behind your fitness goals; and map out and carry out a smart action plan?
* Proper nutrition is a major part of one's overall fitness level. What do you eat? How do you prepare your food? Where do you shop?

Fitness depends on mental discipline. It's not so much about how we measure up to the person next to us in the weight room. In short, when and if you consider a fitness program, understand why you are doing it, surround yourself with appropriate and healthy resources, stay focused and safe, and strengthen your resilience along the way.

Consideration, Conversation, & Collaboration

❧

* Let's expand on this quote: "How do you walk around in something you were born with and not know anything about it or not be aware of what affects it?" Consider it from your community perspective: "How do you *live* in *a place* and not know anything about it or not be aware of what affects it?" What do you need to be more aware of in your community? How have you come to this awareness?
* As you look to the future and consider your community membership and goals, what new or improved resources will you need?
* What does your community do to promote well-being? What new resources does it need to consider?
* What other questions do you need to address regarding this topic?

Leadership as a Resource[85]

❦

IN THE *FAST COMPANY* 2016 Leadership Issue[86] the article "Lessons of Leadership" presented key takeaways learned and shared at the inaugural *Fast Company Innovation Festival*.

As you read the selected insights below, consider how both your community's and your personal experiences and perceptions compare to the leaders' views on trust, failure, innovation, listening, possibilities, and self-limiting constraints.

Maybe you don't wish to measure up; maybe you do. Their experiences offer points for consideration. In their words (**bold-faced** highlights are my emphasis), here are a few lessons for leadership, collaboration, and community building:

- "In the work environment, **innovation comes from great trust, from people having a voice. Fear inhibits innovation.**"-Susan Reilly Salgado (Union Square Hospitality)
- "The difference between **skill and talent**: A skill is something you learn. Talent is what you can't help doing."-Caroline Gibson (Levo)
- "Don't be afraid to fail, but when you do, **fail fast and laugh at yourself.**" Michael Houston (Grey North America)
- "As exciting as the digital age is, the most brilliant, fastest tech can't bring what **human connection** can bring." Jim Brett (West Elm)

- "First of all, just **listen and learn**."-Angela Ahrendts (Apple)
- "If you make **something you love**, people are going to fall in love with it."-Brown Johnson (Sesame Workshop)
- "**Learn**. Know what you didn't know before."-Eileen Fisher (Eileen Fisher, Inc)
- "It's the hypothesis that **there's nothing sacred that can't be changed**....If you just think about the world of **possibilities** with the existing infrastructure, you're massively limiting yourself....There's something beautiful about **ignoring all realistic constraints**."-Anne Wokcicki (23andMe)

Ahrendts of Apple (and previously of Burberry) emphasized that when we listen, we build trust, and the people we lead want to collaborate. The followers gladly follow and go beyond being clock punchers. She cited that Apple's retention rate among employees hit 81% "because they felt connected." And the effective leaders and teams have "emotional electricity."

Every two weeks the Atlantic Beach, Florida, City Commission convenes to discuss the business of our community. The public can address our elected representatives. The Speaker Request Form includes this reminder as to what respect means:

Refrain from put downs, criticism and personal attacks.
Encourage others to state their views.
Support each other, even if you don't agree.
Practice active listening.
Express yourself assertively not aggressively, not submissively.
Collaborate, do not compete or collude.
Trust each other, unless and until such trust is violated.

Consideration, Conversation, & Collaboration

❧

* Consider a 360-degree evaluation[87] of your community's leadership. Bring a cross-section of members together to determine the scope and process. What resources can help you with this type of evaluation?
* What failure did your community recently experience? Was this because of a lack of resources, a failure to use existing resources, a breakdown of resources, or some other factor related to resources? What lessons evolved?
* Fully explain at least three resources and/or processes that your community has that empowers and connects the members to the community's growth and resilience.
* What other questions do you need to address regarding this topic?

The Power of Networking[88]

I HAVE ATTENDED AND/OR FACILITATED hundreds of conference sessions and workshops during my career. These collective gatherings have brought together thousands of professionals from down the hall and those from around the world to discuss critical issues.

National, regional, and local programs provide a network for collegiality that is hard to duplicate. It allows us to move away from our insular communities on the work campus to connect and share with colleagues from around the nation.

True, in the age of social media, we can Skype, Hangout, Zoom, and chat. But there is still nothing quite like the feeling of shaking a colleague's hand, taking time for a cup of coffee, and looking into one another's eyes. It can provide personal validation, opportunities for social integration, and a sense of professional relevance.

When I first got into higher education, a colleague of mine constantly encouraged me to attend professional development opportunities. I typically dismissed his suggestion with the explanation that I did not need to take the time from my campus culture. I believed my work responsibilities could only be addressed and advanced with me onsite. Over the years, though, I came to understand and appreciate my older colleague's wisdom and my then-myopic view of personal and professional development.

When I was on the road, I took the opportunity to connect my students with the places and events I had the good fortune to visit. I started a *series* called "Where in the World is Professor P?" I shot on location a (usually) 90-second video that asked students to guess my whereabouts. I used questions (pop culture, history, geography, sports, and the like) as clues.

I came to understand a collateral benefit of these videos when one of my international students told me that my videos inspired her to continue her education because she wanted to be able to travel like me. In a small way, my attendance at an out-of-town conference helped connect my students to a larger world and make their college dreams more relevant.

I cannot over-estimate what I received professionally and personally from these off-site events. I constantly learned, built networks, and strengthened long-time connections while forging new ones.

It takes more than exchanging an email address, a business card, or a tweet to build meaningful connections. Do what you can to be an agent of collegiality and collaboration.

Consideration, Conversation, & Collaboration

❦

- What do you and your community do to build internal and external connections, resources, and support systems?
- What can your community do to develop its own home-grown conference? What issues would benefit from a half-day or full-day conference? What would the agenda look like? Who would speak and facilitate? Who will be on your planning committee?
- If you do not have the resources to start your own event, what nearby events (in other communities) would you benefit from attending? How would your attendance benefit your community?
- Perhaps you could have a coffee hour at one of the neighbor's homes and have a guest speaker talk about ways to build community. Who would the invited speaker be for such an event? When will you send the invitation?
- What other questions do you need to address regarding this topic?

A Deeper Dive: VPEER

❧

For this exercise, focus on two communities with which you have membership. One should be a vibrant and prospering community. The other ranks amongst the weakest. Name each one below.

My strongest community is _____.

My weakest community is _____.

Now, for each community answer the questions below.

* **Visualize** the purpose, journey, and membership of your community. What *weak signals* exist to indicate the future of your community will not look like the past? What does this future focus tell you? What does the community you envision look like?
* **Prioritize** the resources you will need, and the actions required to sustain your community—and make it thrive into the future. What non-negotiable steps do you need to take? What comes first? How will you prioritize **RESOURCES** to help build and strengthen your community?
* **Exorcise** that which no longer serves or nourishes your community. How can you minimize or eliminate the pernicious effects? Where does this fit with your prioritization of resources and actions? Who will help you identify these factors? Where will this fit in your prioritization?
* **Exercise** and strengthen the emotional, physical, and spiritual dimensions of life. Community building can be challenging work. How will you and your members build and maintain a healthy life style moving forward? Where can you find this on your list of priorities?

- **Realize** your visualization. How often will you stop to evaluate your progress? How will you realize if you are faithfully following the four steps above (visualize, prioritize, exorcise, and exercise)?

Rainbows

One's dreams, goals, desires, and vision connect to one's overall journey.

❧❧❧

RELATED TERMS INCLUDE: ACTION, CHANGE, core values, failure, fitness, goals, priorities, relationships, resources, risk, and *vulnerability.*[89]

A TRANSFORMATIONAL STORY ABOUT COMMUNITY: "MENTORS FOR MUSIC, HOPE, & RAINBOWS"

Research tells us that *hope* requires three ingredients: goals + pathways + agency.[90] The goal—a rainbow that attracts and draws your attention—must be valuable to you and/or your community. A pathway—a plausible route to the goal—must be present. And, you intuit that you have the ability, the power, and the talent to reach that goal.

Mentors can assist along the pathway. They can help us discover the agency we have not yet recognized in ourselves. We may think of mentors as solo entities, individuals sharing expertise. If one mentor, however, can change a life, think what a community of mentors can do. That's what the Atlantic Beach, Florida, Songwriters' Night has provided since 2003.

The Songwriters' Night (SWN) started on the back of a cocktail napkin. In 2003, after the Atlantic Beach Cultural Arts and Recreation Advisory Committee approved my suggestion for the city to sponsor an outdoor music event for our community, I went to the best person I knew who could deliver as both the MC and musical muse for the event, Mike

Shack Shackelford. As a singer-songwriter, Shack brought the musical chops needed to produce a professional event. He could mentor me (as the promoter) and the stage performers as well.

At the time, Shack's band was playing at a lounge in Atlantic Beach. I met him there one night and our plan came together in a matter of minutes. With the support of our city government, we would provide a free, family-friendly music event for our community. It would be for amateurs and professionals alike. No auditions required. All welcomed. Respectful performances (read: G-rated; family-oriented) only.

We hoped to be a pathway for our community members. A pathway for songwriters to share their talents, gain confidence, and connect with like-minded creative types. It would also be a pathway for the audience. Neighbors entertaining neighbors while enjoying the company of other neighbors. And for some of the performers, SWN might become one step toward a larger goal—a personal Rainbow—related to music, songwriting, and performing.

Over the years, the adults have shared the stage with children of the community. These young artists test and hone their musical skills in a true listening-room environment.

One such aspiring singer-songwriter shared her experiences with me. Twelve-year old Izzy Moon Mayforth told me she likes that people listen to her music—and that she gets to listen to others and learn from them about her songwriting and performing. When she hears the heartfelt applause after her performances, she says to herself, "Glad that I did it!" She gains confidence—and that fuels personal agency.[91]

Shack believes one of the beautiful results of the monthly events is to see people, who were reticent at first, come back as part of the regular rotation of artists. Another is to watch young artists grow. One such performer helped me with his vocals and a tasteful guitar lead as we performed one of my songs. He was about ten years old. By the time he tuned 17, he was winning awards for his music in Hollywood and around the country. Today, he records and acts in Los Angeles.[92]

For the audience, the event exemplifies the concept of *social capital*. It serves as a community laboratory to help all ages, of varying abilities, to chase down their dreams. In between songs, before the event, or after the lights go dark, the audience talks about things other than music like neighborhood schools, workplace opportunities, home improvement projects, or important community issues. Spin-off events to other parts of the county have occurred as well.

A beach venue for dreams helps create a pathway for other such venues.

And hope lives. When people take time to listen to and give gratitude for the gifts of others, community strengthens. As Izzy sings in one of her original compositions,[93] "You're my friend, and I love you."

Before You Start

❧

OFTEN, WE CONSIDER DREAMS TO be personal. Our communities have dreams as well. It could be for complete streets, access to fresh food and medical care, or transparent connections with our leaders. Maybe those dreams involve a revitalized workspace. Dreams provide hope. Hope needs pathways and agency for realization.

Consider communities—vibrant as well as those that struggle—to which you belong. How can the concept of **RAINBOWS** help the vibrant ones prosper and the struggling ones grow?

For instance, think of a dynamic community to which you belong. In what ways do the **RAINBOWS** in that community contribute to its growth and resilience? Conversely, what do your struggling communities lack when it comes to **RAINBOWS**?

Below you will find blog post excerpts related to the concept of **RAINBOWS**. Choose one, read it, and consider its message. You will probably note that one or more of the other Seven Rs come into play as well. These core values mutually reinforce one another. Begin a conversation about how you and your community can use the points to foster and sustain community.

Then, repeat with the other blog excerpts.

After each excerpt you will find several suggestions and specific questions on how to bring the teachings of the piece to life in your community. Rather than settling for general answers, use the following three-step model to help you be more actionable with your responses.

1. Establish a realistic, feasible, time-bound plan for implementing your proposed actions.
2. Execute your plan. Make sure all involved understand their roles and responsibilities.
3. Evaluate your progress on a regular basis. Adjust course as needed.

Where Do We Go Next?[94]

❧

We are where we are, however we got here.
What matters is where we go next.

—ISAAC MARION

WE GENERALLY HEAR GOAL STATEMENTS or sentiments accompanied by words and phrases such as *intention, focus, the best year ever, the dawn of a new you, we'll see what happens,* and *this year's gotta be better than last.* We also hear of *to do* lists for the coming year. Richard Branson urges people to ditch that list with a *to be* list.[95]

Our choices have moved us to where we are. And our next choice will take us toward where we want to be. Where we go next depends on what we do now. Today really is the tomorrow we created yesterday.

If we don't like our today, perhaps we would do well to evaluate what we did yesterday. And the day before that. And before that. And then zero in on where we go next—tomorrow. I've heard athletes say they quickly put a failure (strikeout, interception, missed game-winning shot) behind them and focus on the next at bat, play, or run down the court.

Obviously, events happen to us. Injustice occurs. Cancer arrives uninvited. Death appears arbitrary. A natural disaster takes everything a family or community owns. An election turns a nation on its collective heads. In those situations, it appears disingenuous to say "focus on the journey" or "your yesterday got you to today."

For sure, you and your community are where you are. Just as certain, you and your neighbors will go where you purposefully take yourself. Or, you could wait to be carried along on your journey by negative, pessimistic, fearful, and myopic minds. Your choice.

Events, people, or circumstances do play a role in our journey. So, does our response.

Consideration, Conversation, & Collaboration

☙

* Where do you and your community wish to go next? What goals have you and your leaders set for the coming year?
* How did you arrive at the above goals—collaboration or dictation?
* What relationships and resources will you and your community need to move toward your goals?
* What steps have you put in place for periodic evaluation and re-calibration as you move toward the goals?
* What other questions do you need to address regarding this topic?

Stories You Tell Yourself[96]

❧

FOR YEARS I'VE BEEN USING a professional and personal growth exercise with students and other audiences.

* Start with one piece of paper and a pen.
* Draw a line down the center of the page.
* At the top of the left column write the word PRIORITIES and at the top of the right column write the word TIME.
* In the PRIORITIES column list the three things that are the most valuable or the biggest priorities in your life right now.
* In the TIME column list the three things that take most of your time each week.
* The final step ends up being the eye-opener: When you look at what you say you value and how and where you use your time, do you see any disconnections?

All of us can talk about what is important. When it comes to walking our talk, though, do our actions match what we say?

The PRIORITIES column represents our intentions; the stories we tell ourselves about what we value. The TIME column indicates the stories we live.

Inspired by Tony Schwartz's book *The Way We're Working Isn't Working*, I added a third step to the exercise.

Go back to the two-column page and do the following:

* In the PRIORITIES column, rate how important in your life each item is. Use the scale of 1 (not particularly important) to 10 (extremely important).
* In the TIME column, rate how much of week is devoted to this stated value or intention. Again, use the scale of 1 (nearly no time) to 10 (a great deal of time).
* Add a third column and label it DISCONNECTION.
* Subtract the number you wrote in column 2 from the number you wrote in column 1. This is your DISCONNECTION between intention and reality.

The bigger the disconnection, the more work you need to do. The *work* could be a re-evaluation of what you *demonstrate* to be a value as opposed to what you *say* you value. Or it could be a re-commitment to your stated priorities by re-arranging the way you spend or invest your time.

Several years ago I did the above exercise with a group of students. One young woman became perturbed with the exercise. She announced to the class, "I don't like your activity!"

When pressed as to why, she said her job took most of her time each week—and she hated her job. "According to you," she blurted, "I should value my job."

I said, "If you hate your job that much, why don't you quit?"

She informed me that as a single mother she needed the money her job provided for necessities of life.

I offered that it appeared the job was indeed valuable to her, a huge priority. The exercise did not ask what she liked—but what she valued. She was telling herself one story while living another story.

Sometimes the exercise can clearly show a misalignment of priorities and time. Maybe you list your spouse or partner as your number one priority. However, in the TIME column, he/she does not crack the top ten. Is he/she really your number one priority?

You might place losing weight and getting into shape at the top of the PRIORITY column. Nowhere on the TIME side, though, can you see any exercise noted.

Such cases allow us the opportunity to have a conversation with ourselves about what we really value—and why we do what we do. A mentor can be a valuable resource to help you sort through discrepancies you may find.

What stories do you tell yourself? What stories do you live?

Consideration, Conversation, & Collaboration

* Consider your community. What are the top three priorities you see for your community?
* When it comes to advancing the spirit of your community, what three activities take most of your and your neighbors' time?
* To what degree do you find connections or disconnections?
* What other questions do you need to address regarding this topic?

Invite The Right People On Your Journey[97]

❦

A MOTHER WRITES A LETTER[98] to her daughters offering the following advice:

...Stay in your lane...the path will illuminate itself
so long as you stay present,
open to the signs, and follow your passions.
It's all related.

Be true to yourself. Be mindful. Be open.

Not only do we need to be present when it comes to our passions and curiosity, we must be mindful of who we allow on the journey. Three *types* of fellow travelers can have widely disparate influences on your path. You may have read about them and encountered them yourself.

The *No-Goes*.[99] These folks will get in your way, attempt to block you, and tell you things can't be done the way you envision them. They may want to control you. Maybe they fear your progress bodes ill for them. Or they may be fearful and reticent types, always remaining in their self-defined narrow limits. They seem to hold their breath a lot while they scan the horizon searching for lions, and tigers, and bears. Oh, my!

The *Slow-Goes*. They will not out-and-out block you, but they remain so tentative they can get in your way. They may not throw obstacles at you like their stifling cousins the No-Goes, but that wet blanket they toss around your shoulders slows your momentum nonetheless. Happy to plod along, our slow-go friends don't make much progress, kind of stuck in second gear. While they don't hold their breath, you may see them hyperventilating often.

The *Go-Goes.* Consider these the early adopters of life, its wonders, and ever-present opportunities. They innovate for themselves and inspire others. They thrive on movement, experimentation, and evaluated feedback. They risk vulnerability and failure. They breathe deeply and live life.

Caution: Not every No-Go or Slow-Go should be considered an antagonist to shun, or an anchor to cast off. At times, each can provide valuable and prudent counsel. A trusted mentor, a wise friend, and thoughtful family members may have needed perspective you lack. Listen, however, with all your senses. Consider carefully.

And we must understand our role with others. That is, do we serve as No-Goes, Slow-Goes, or Go-Goes for other people's aspirations? Do we help or hinder? Do we encourage or suffocate?

In his book *Before Happiness,* author Shawn Achor points out that our brains process millions upon millions of bits of information each day.[100] We only attend to a miniscule fraction of these stimuli. His research shows, however, that we usually attend to the same kind of information and ignore the alternatives or contradictory data. Think about people who, no matter how sunny it is, always focus on that one cloud on the horizon. Where we see brightness, they see potential—nay, impending—doom. We have a choice.

This week pay attention to your goals. Be mindful of whom you let influence your travels and let into your mind. Sometimes we *no-go* ourselves because of fear. It might not be as scary as it looks. Where is the edge of your comfort zone?

Consideration, Conversation, & Collaboration

❦

* As you survey your community, who are the No-Goes, Slow-Goes, and Go-Goes?
* In which category (No-Goes, Slow-Goes, and Go-Goes) do you place yourself most of the time? What evidence do you have?
* How can No-Goes and Slow-Goes serve a beneficial role in your community? How can you learn from them?
* Identify one project in your community that sits outside of the collective comfort zone. What can you do this week to act on this project—turn it from talk to an initiative? Who on your team is the best suited to help with this movement?
* What other questions do you need to address regarding this topic?

We Can Walk a Pathway & Never See it at All[101]

✦

WALKING ALONG A STREET IN Boulder, Colorado, I almost missed the bunny rabbit sitting three feet in front of me.

I had a similar experience a few days later when I passed a wild deer munching on grass behind the University of Colorado practice football field alongside the Boulder Creek.

Each time, I was following the path. And each time, I almost missed the journey.

Thomas Cleary in *No Barrier: Unlocking the Zen Koan*, shares two simple yet eloquent truisms about life:

> *Just reading a map is not making the journey,*
> *but without reading the map there is no direction.*

and

> *Those in a hurry do not arrive.*

There can be a lot of distractions along the daily paths we trod. When we become caught up in the external and/or internal distractions we miss the signs and beauty right in front, beside, behind, above, or beneath us. A beautiful sunrise or a bunny and a deer.

We can be consumed by habit, patterns of thought, routines, and perseveration that we miss signs and guideposts. Yes, we need to read the map, but just because we read it does not a journey make.

We can walk a pathway and never see it at all.

Consideration, Conversation, & Collaboration

⬥ The next time you walk through your community pause and look. Really look. What beauty have you taken for granted?

⬥ The next time you walk through your community pause and look. Really look. What areas of concern have you overlooked?

⬥ What and/or who distracts your community from the real business it needs to tend to at this point?

⬥ What weak signals from the future indicate your community may need to follow a different path?

⬥ What other questions do you need to address regarding this topic?

You Need To Be There, & You Need To Be There![102]

❧

As a professor, I was responsible for creating well-thought out lessons that engaged and challenged my students. The students, as well, had the responsibility to be active participants in the classroom. It was a choreographed dance. In "The Load Out(Stay)," Jackson Browne sings,

People you've got the power over what we do.
You can sit there and wait, or you can pull us through.
Come along, sing the song. You know you can't go wrong….

The collective personalities of my classes ran high with enthusiasm and curiosity. Most students showed excitement for the material and their classmates. In short, they "could pull us through" to great heights. I would like to think I had something to do with that energy. As any teacher can attest, there are those classes in which the students do "sit there and wait." And, I guess, I had something to do with that as well.

I told my students, "Not only do *you need to be here* in class, *you need to be here* in class." The students' physical presence was important as it allowed them to hear explanations, ask questions, and add to the class discussions. Their attention, thoughts, and heads needed to be focused on the class lesson, as well. I used the following checklist to help students move toward a more active and successful life in school—and beyond. I encouraged them to internalize the lists and grow with them.[103] The same goes for the workplace or a community meeting. Below you will find a brief example for classrooms and the workplace. Add an example that pertains to your community.

- ● ***Do you show up?*** Pretty basic, isn't it? In a way, punctuality shows that you have control of your world.
  - ● Classroom. It's difficult to meet instructor expectations if you're sitting in the student lounge or asleep in your bed during class time.
  - ● Workplace. How do you know what your boss or client wants or expects if you don't attend the latest strategy briefing?
- ● ***Do you bring all you need?***
  - ● Classroom. This is not the time to be without paper, pen, textbook, laptop, or tablet.
  - ● Workplace. Do you have the quarterly report? Have you reviewed the minutes from the last meeting? Are you expected to have updated statistics about customers?
- ● ***Do you arrive on time?*** Again, basic. Classes and business meetings generally have a recognized starting and ending time. Think of a movie. If you come in late or leave early, you will miss critical scenes that will hinder your understanding of the entire film.
  - ● Classroom. Many instructors orchestrate each moment of class.
  - ● Workplace. Same for your supervisor, the weekly staff meeting, or monthly lunch-and-learn. The meeting has a *start* time for a reason.
- ● ***Do you sit where you will benefit the most?***
  - ● Classroom. To minimize distractions, you may wish to sit close to where the instructor or speaker is standing. Unless you have been given explicit instructions to access your social media sites, this is not the time to text message, check for updates, or view videos.

* Workplace. Sitting with your current project team members, for instance, will allow you to discuss meeting topics as they pertain to your work.
* ***Do you carry your passion with you?*** Be excited!
    * Classroom. Whether you sit in a required class for your major or an elective class to fill out your schedule, bring as much excitement for each meeting and content as you can. This can be as simple as coming in with one authentic and thoughtful question about the homework reading. Remember that you are a participant in the teaching and learning dynamic.
    * Workplace. Think of the *No-Goes* you have encountered in your career; the negative people who never wanted to move forward with anything. Can you remember how they sucked the air out of the room? This is your chance to bring life to a meeting or initiative.
* ***Do you remain actively engaged?***
    * Classroom. Practice your active listening skills. Listen intently; ask probing questions; be involved. Especially for classes that present challenges to you, participating can help you stay focused and engaged. This in turn can help comprehension.
    * Workplace. Ask intentional questions. That is, go beyond the obvious and take a deeper dive to seek clarification or expansion of ideas as needed. Understand what is expected of you and your team before you leave the meeting.
* ***Do you review your notes as soon as possible?***
    * Classroom and Workplace. If you have the time, complete this review before you leave the room. Remain for a few moments and quickly determine whether you have any questions or confusion about the session material. Or find a quiet place as soon as possible to complete your review. Maybe a cup of coffee with a friend can help debrief the staff meeting.

* ***Do you act with civility?*** Remind yourself about decorum.
    * Classroom. Develop an appropriate civil relationship with professors and classmates. You will be spending a few months of your life with them. Treat them with the respect you expect. Challenge your assumptions you may have about people in the classroom.[104]
    * Workplace. Develop an appropriate civil relationship with supervisors and colleagues. Turn off the cell phone and listen to the person speaking. Communicate and connect with those in the room. If a new employee is present, introduce yourself and offer to introduce her to other people in the meeting. Greet colleagues with a hearty "Hello!" and smile. Even when there is disagreement, civility may help pave the way to understanding and collaboration.

Consideration, Conversation, & Collaboration

❧

* As you review the eight *Do* steps above, which do you find missing in your community meetings? Why do you think that is the case? Which do you follow?
* What *Do* step would you add to this list?
* I have reduced the above items to a brief video, "Study Skills: Success Strategies for the Classroom."[105] While the video addresses classroom success, the steps have broad applicability. What other questions do you need to address regarding this topic?

Comfort Zones: The Good & Not-So-Good[106]

❧

WHEN ROXIE ARRIVED IN OUR lives as a 14-week old rescue puppy, she immediately began teaching us.

As a new member of the family, she often retreated to two areas—two comfort zones. Whether it was her crate with chew toys or her comfy stuffed cushion by my desk, she felt solace in each area. She ventured out to explore a room, tentatively looking this way and that. And then, returned to one of her comfort zones. Outside she staked claim to her new yard and then back to the comfort zones to catch her breath. With each venture outside the zone, she gained more confidence and a bounce in her step.

She reminded me that we all have comfort zones. Those areas of refuge that provide shelter from life's storms can give us pause to reflect on what we do and where we go. A comfort zone can help us gain awareness and begin to recognize and challenge assumptions as we make plans for future action.

Comfort zones, also, can stymie our growth. Consider what would have happened to Roxie if she never left her crate or ventured from her comfy dog couch. She'd miss a whole world of adventure and growth opportunities. She would never have stretched and strengthened her legs. She would have squandered her potential. Each time she stepped out she increased her vulnerability and her chances for development and a fuller life. Roxie, like us, had to assess the risk of each move or non-move.

Thanks to Roxie, two comfort zone lessons emerge.

* Comfort zones provide shelter and opportunities to breathe. When the world has become too crazy to handle, we can retreat from the stresses that, at times, beat us down. They can rejuvenate us.
* A comfort zone can become a crutch and excuse not to venture out, not to risk, and not to grow. Type the following words into an internet search engine: "Life begins at the end of your comfort zone." You will find, quotes, books, and videos espousing this growth mantra.

Pay attention at your next staff meeting. Do people gravitate to the same seats they have every time they come to the room? Do they sit with the same people? At the college, I had colleagues who only wanted to teach the same courses at the same times of the same days each semester. Change created angst. When a new leader takes over an organization, people make arguments as to why their part of the world should be protected. Comfort zones.

As you approach the coming week consider your comfort zones. Be grateful you have these places where you can de-stress and catch your breath. And consider what steps you can take to venture a bit further from their confines, so you can embrace new adventures and growth opportunities.

Consideration, Conversation, & Collaboration

❧

- Does your community have comfort zones for members? Where are they located? Where could they be located? What factors make them comfort zones?

- Consider a neighborhood reading circle. One work to consider and discuss with your neighbors is *The Abundant Community: Awakening the Power of Families and Neighborhoods* by John McKnight and Peter Block. Who would be an effective leader for this reading circle? When can you start?

- McKnight and Block reference the "garage syndrome." This is when people exit their garages each morning, drive to work, and then return from work, pull into their garages, shut the door, and enter their homes. Interaction with neighbors is minimal at best. The garage and house become comfort zones, safely separating residents from residents. Does your community suffer from the garage syndrome? Do neighbors enter and exist their homes through their garages, seldom interacting with their neighbors? How does this affect community spirit and strength?

- What other questions do you need to address regarding this topic?

Possibilities[107]

❧

ON APRIL 8, 2012, BUBBA Watson won the Masters Tournament at Augusta, Georgia. A shot from the rough alongside the fairway instantly became golfing lore. The announcer reminded us that Bubba had never taken a golf lesson or *parsed his swing* from a video. Those who know the game might call him *a golfing natural.*

All of this makes for compelling human interest and even for non-golfers, his story connected. One statement from his post-tournament Green Jacket interview grabbed me. Bubba said, "I never got this far in my dream."

Just a couple days before Bubba's improbable victory, I had said to a friend at lunch something similar—but not quite as eloquently. The gist of my thought was simple. If you were to have asked me 20 years ago to articulate my professional dream, there is no way I would have told you that in those 20 years I would become a professor, author, speaker, and songwriter. I never got that far in my dream.

For me, that represented an enormous realization. One of my writing and teaching themes is encapsulated in two questions:

*   What is your dream?
*   What are doing to get to your dream?

We can plan. We can gather our resources. And we can analyze every little piece of decisions we make. And we can end up missing the dream.

We don't know when we will end up in the rough or the trees as Bubba did on that last hole. If we stay focused and true to our journey, we will find ways forward.

Do not shut down your future. Some people get to a point where they have reached their envisioned dream—and then stop there. You could call it *plateauing*. Bubba put a new twist on it for me.

Do we ever know when we have reached the dream? Are they dreams or endpoints or benchmarks?

Consider the reminders to stay open to the possibilities of where our dreams can lead us. And, to live passionately.

Consideration, Conversation, & Collaboration

* What milestone has your community most recently reached?
* What is the next milestone your community needs to reach?
* What relationships and resources will be able to help your community reach this milestone?
* Is your community, using a golfing metaphor, *in the rough*? Can you describe the situation or issue? What and who can lead the way forward?
* What other questions do you need to address regarding this topic?

A Deeper Dive: VPEER

❧

For this exercise, focus on two communities with which you have membership. One should be a vibrant and prospering community. The other ranks amongst the weakest. Name each one below.

My strongest community is _____.

My weakest community is _____.

Now, for each community answer the questions below.

* **Visualize** the purpose, journey, and membership of your community. What *weak signals* exist to indicate the future of your community will not look like the past? What does this future focus tell you? What does the community you envision look like?
* **Prioritize** the resources you will need, and the actions required to sustain your community—and make it thrive into the future. What non-negotiable steps do you need to take? What comes first? How will you prioritize **RAINBOWS** to help build and strengthen your community?
* **Exorcise** that which no longer serves or nourishes your community. How can you minimize or eliminate the pernicious effects? Where does this fit with your prioritization of resources and actions? Who will help you identify these factors? Where will this fit in your prioritization?
* **Exercise** and strengthen the emotional, physical, and spiritual dimensions of life. Community building can be challenging work. How will you and your members build and maintain a healthy lifestyle moving forward? Where can you find this on your list of priorities?

* **Realize** your visualization. How often will you stop to evaluate your progress? How will you realize if you are faithfully following the four steps above (visualize, prioritize, exorcise, and exercise)?

Responsibility

Acting in a manner that connects to virtue and in accordance with one's core values.

❧

RELATED TERMS INCLUDE: ACTION, ACCOUNTABILITY, authenticity, change, core values, critical thinking, excuses, goals, integrity, procrastination, purpose, and *vulnerability.*[108]

A TRANSFORMATIONAL STORY ABOUT COMMUNITY: "HELPING A VILLAGE FIND ITS VOICE"

Without a vision, a nation perishes.

—Proverbs 29:18

If you have built castles in the air, your work need not be lost;
that is where they should be. Now put
the foundation under them.

—ATTRIBUTED TO HENRY DAVID THOREAU

Just giving voice to our dreams can be the motivating first step needed to move a specific goal into the realm of reality. On our way to realization, we need to go from visualization to verbalization, and, finally, to transformation. Dreams without action quickly become fantasies.

When our community looks toward its rainbows—its dreams—the members see all manner of hope and possibility. Whether they seem impossibly distant or close at hand, we need to marshal strength, energy, and resources to move forward. The community members must step up and take responsibility for vision and actions.

We have heard that the village raises up a child. But what can be done if the village itself needs to be raised up? What do we do, for instance, if the village has inadequate infrastructure, health disparities, high crime and poverty, lack of accessible pharmacies and fresh foods, and educational and financial literacy challenges? Threatened on many levels, the village nears the breaking point. If you're George Maxey, you listen and help the villagers create a movement.

Maxey has served as the Executive Director of the New Town Success Zone (NTSZ) in Jacksonville, Florida, since 2015. Brought to life in 2008 with the help of the Jacksonville Children's Commission, NTSZ serves an area of about 3,000 people in a small (one-to two-mile) geographic zone. Sitting in his office[109] at the Center for the Prevention of Health Disparities at Edward Waters College, Maxey told me about the importance of keeping people connected to their dreams, aspirations, and hopes. While no one needed to remind the residents about the realities they faced, the challenge remained to address those realities and grow as a neighborhood.

You see, the NTSZ lacked basic resources. For instance, the nearest pharmacy was two miles away and the neighborhood was a food desert. The local discount store did not carry fresh fruits and vegetables. This in turn affected diet, nutrition, and health. Nevertheless, the founding director (the person before Maxey) reminded the neighbors they could reach their goals. Their personal and neighborhood rainbows were more than fantasies, he told them. If they worked to achieve those dreams they would create their reality.

Maxey carried that message forward. He also realized the neighbors must organize to be heard. They had to create a movement and "build infrastructure and social capital for neighborhoods with significant disparities." Among other things, he wanted to hear what the residents had to say about the lingering health disparities in the NTSZ. He gathered the community *gatekeepers* (the de facto leaders). And he listened. And he learned. More importantly, he gave the neighbors a platform to develop and share their collective voice. What were their community goals?

People must have a say-so about what is going on in their community if change is to take root.

Maxey asked the gatekeepers, "Where do you want to see the community go? What are you willing to do to get what you need to be successful?"

Dreams[110] give us direction. To move toward the dreams, we need to act. Our actions (or inactions) create our reality.

The same goes for a community.

The neighbors told Maxey when the basics of the physical infrastructure like trash pickup, sidewalks, lighting, and blight challenge daily life, it becomes difficult to focus on, let alone tackle, personal health issues. Think Maslow's Hierarchy of Needs.

Maxey asked himself, "How can I organize the community to have that voice?"

He helped form the Vision Keepers who "do the work required to ensure that the children and the families are making adequate progress towards success." They held themselves accountable.

They collaborated with the Jacksonville Sheriff's Office. They invited their city council representative to neighborhood meetings. They involved HabiJax, the Jacksonville Habitat for Humanity. The Vision Keepers understood that for the NTSZ to grow, the *official* leadership of the city had to understand their needs. Not by yelling or threatening, but by respecting, educating, and supporting the leadership. Speaking. Sharing. Listening.

We can all learn from this civil, respectful approach to focus on responsibility for one's self, family, and community.

After a decade of existence, NTSZ boasts sustainable and transformative initiatives in the areas of:

* Education
  * Includes the two-generation approach to educate vulnerable children and their caregivers.

- Community Capacity and Sustainability
  - Includes development of entrepreneurship and leadership skills.
- Social Well-being
  - Includes a community garden and wellness workshops.
- Employment
  - Includes a career and personal finance center.

Today the glue—the core value—of forming and maintaining respectful and responsible relationships holds this community of strong neighbors together. They keep sustainability foremost in view. Neighbors assume the responsibility to train neighbors. Maxey believes part of their success comes from their neighbor-to-neighbor focus. It is not about one leader. "We want everyone to be part of the leading process," he said.

Listen and respect one another.

Find your voice.

Use your voice.

Pursue your rainbows.

And do it all in the name of something bigger than yourself.

This week, identify and commit to doing one thing that will get one of your communities closer to one of its dreams. Ben Franklin reportedly reminded us long ago that "Energy and persistence conquer all things."

Before You Start

CONSIDER COMMUNITIES—VIBRANT AS WELL AS those that struggle—to which you belong. How does **RESPONSIBILITY** help the vibrant ones prosper and the struggling ones grow?

For instance, think of a dynamic community to which you belong. In what ways does **RESPONSIBILITY** in that community contribute to its growth and resilience? Conversely, what do your struggling communities lack when it comes to **RESPONSIBILITY**?

In what ways do your various communities help their members find their respective voices? How effective have your communities been in expecting members to behave responsibly in the pursuit of community goals?

Below you will find blog post excerpts related to the concept of **RESPONSIBILITY**. Choose one, read it, and consider its message. You will probably note that one or more of the other Seven Rs come into play as well. These core values mutually reinforce one another. Begin a conversation about how you and your community can use the points to foster and sustain community.

Then, repeat with the other blog excerpts.

After each excerpt you will find several suggestions and specific questions on how to bring the teachings of the piece to life in your community. Rather than settling for general answers, use the following three-step model to help you be more actionable with your responses.

1. Establish a realistic, feasible, time-bound plan for implementing your proposed actions.
2. Execute your plan. Make sure all involved understand their roles and responsibilities.
3. Evaluate your progress on a regular basis. Adjust course as needed.

Priorities: Five in Your Pocket[111]

❧

WRITE FIVE VALUES THAT ARE important to you on a 3 x 5 index card. Focus on traits and characteristics rather than going for the obvious people (my kids, my spouse, and my friends) or things (my house and my car). For instance, these five came to mind for me:

- Acting with discipline.
- Maintaining well-being.
- Making a difference.
- Being dependable.
- Demonstrating kindness.

Put the card in your pocket and for the next week note how many times you act on your values. Do your actions reflect your stated values?

Some weeks I am on target. Others it appears that someone else made up my list. I am a work in progress.

This strategy provides a nudge or reminder we might need to focus on and practice what we say we value. It can remind us of our self-identified responsibilities.

Understand your values—and live those values each day.

Consideration, Conversation, & Collaboration

❧

* What values rank as the top five for your community? How do you know?
* For each value, list one instance of when it was acted upon in your community? What resulted from this action?
* Look at each value, can you think of a time when the community came up short on this value? Why did that happen?
* View "Your Effort Matters: Thank You!"[112] from one of my keynote addresses to remind your community that "Your Effort Matters."
* What other questions do you need to address regarding this topic?

Dreams. Action. Reality![113]

❧

ON ONE OF MY SUNRISE beach walks, I passed a surfer sitting on the sand looking at the ocean like a football player getting his game face on. "The waves don't look as big as I thought they'd be," I said as I passed him.

"Not a problem," he said, "just as long as they're consistent."

Just as long as they're consistent. Marvelous! Isn't that the way it is with teams, relationships, communities, your exercise, and your goals?

I have used the wording "huge outrageous goals." Jim Collins writes about "big hairy audacious goals."[114] Both phrases reference goals that make us reach; that make us stretch; that push us to go just a little bit further. Powerful and important.

I kept thinking about the surfer's word: *Consistent.* And the importance of consistency with our goals—large and small. External consistency: between our goals. Internal consistency: within our goals.

- External consistency. Do your goals complement one another? Or do they work at cross purposes and frustrate you? Goals can be huge, but if they negate your big picture then it really doesn't matter how big they are.
  - Example. John is a student with big dreams for a large life once he gets his college degree. He has enrolled in six classes this term to get to the dream as quickly as possible. He also has a shorter-term goal of owning a car, so he does not have to rely on public transportation. To buy his car outright (he

doesn't want debt—another admirable goal) he is working thirty hours a week on the night shift at an air freight company. He is exhausted and losing his passion and focus for school. His grades have slipped. Last week he was so worn down, he ended up calling in sick two nights in a row. And he missed classes. Two huge (and wonderful) goals start to cancel one another out. They are not consistent with one another.

* Internal consistency. Once you set a goal, do you move forward with consistent action? Are you dedicated to the result—no excuses? Are you intentional with your goals and growth? Or do you just bump along hoping that something magical will happen and transform your goals into reality?

    * Example. Gertie decided to start a blog. "I want to add value and hopefully end up with a book out of it," she told a friend. Gertie read advice and strategies for blogging. A long-time blogger told her to post regularly. Whether it was daily, twice a week, or once a week, she would need to be consistent to attract followers. Gertie decided to do a weekly blog. She was diligent for three weeks—and then she let *stuff* get in the way. Her next post was two weeks later. It is now six weeks since her last post.

Large ideas can certainly create enthusiasm. But absent consistent and responsible action, those big dreams have no legs. They remain fantasies.

Consideration, Conversation, & Collaboration

❦

- What goal does your community need to focus on this week, this month, this quarter, this year?
- What action do you need to take to help the community reach the goal?
- How will you and the members working toward the goal maintain consistent action toward the dream?
- Have you noticed external or internal inconsistencies when it comes to community goals? If you have, what steps will you take to address these inconsistencies?
- What other questions do you need to address regarding this topic?

Three Ideas Worth Practicing[115]

❦

AWARENESS, ASSUMPTIONS, AND ACTIONS. ONCE we understand *what* we do, and *why* we do what we do, we have a better chance to plot an appropriate course of action.

Actions help create our movement for improvement—beyond our limits and toward our potential. Dreams can be great motivators. However, without disciplined and responsible action those dreams will quickly turn to fantasies.

Some students begin their semesters all fired up and ready for action—or so they assume. They have the latest technology, a full load of classes, and they want to reach their finish line as soon as possible. Often, within a few weeks, they run out of gas.

Sometimes we feel like that, too—we lose momentum.

Some students stumble because they lack an awareness of how to *do college*. But more so, there's a question of discipline; a question of *stick-to-it-iveness*. And many times, students are not aware of this.

One study of first-year college students[116] found that nearly one-third self-reported that they either got bored or quit within a few minutes of a study session. About 40% said they did not have a system of personal self-discipline.

Pick one area of your life where you would like to gain a clearer awareness of what you really do. It could be a goal, a challenge, or a full-blown crisis. What would you like to confront? Something that if challenged or embraced will require you to tap into the genius that is already living in your soul. Then answer:

- Are you truly aware of what you do or would like to do in that space? Can you describe it in detail? How do you know what you say you do is what you do? Consider a coach, mentor, good friend or video feedback to help you reflect on your action.
- After you understand what you are doing, ask yourself, "Why do I do what I do? Why do I respond like I do? Why do I act like I do?[117] What values underlie my actions?" Are you validating your *self* or are you betraying your *self*? Once you know exactly what and why you do what you do, then you have a better chance to plot an effective course of action.

We need to move from preparing for action to creating action. And that requires discipline and commitment to make those constant little adjustments necessary that are the prelude to serious action and then lead us on our movement to improvement. Ask yourself again how you know this is the correct course for you. Does it align with your values? It has been said what we think we become. Let's take that one step further: What we do, we become.

Awareness. Assumptions. Actions. Let those become the three ideas worth practicing in your life.

Consideration, Conversation, & Collaboration

❧

* Consider a challenge confronting one of your communities. Describe the challenge. With a small focus group, answer the following questions about the challenge:
    * Awareness. How do you know this is truly a challenge? How did you become aware of this challenge? Who or what does it affect in the community?
    * Assumptions. Why do you believe this challenge exists? As you discuss the challenge with community members, do they see the same challenge and reasons for its existence?
    * Actions. What actions does the community need to take to address or eliminate this challenge? Who can help? Who can lead? When will you start?
* My TEDx presentation addresses "Awareness, Assumptions, and Actions: Why Do We Do What We Do?"[118]
* What other questions do you need to address regarding this topic?

Cogs & Linchpins[119]

❦

THINK ABOUT THE ORGANIZATIONAL MISSION and goals for your workplace. How many of your co-workers know the mission statement and goals? Even the folks who served on the drafting committee probably forgot those words soon after the committee disbanded. I remember a mentor of mine telling me long ago that, even in the business world, mission statements end up long-forgotten in a notebook on a shelf.

At one point in my teaching career, the college challenged the faculty, staff, and administration to inspire our students to make a lifetime commitment to the following values:

* continued learning,
* informed civic engagement,
* ethical leadership,
* cultural appreciation,
* social responsibility, and
* multicultural awareness in an interconnected world.

If those words simply remained on a wall in the board room, they would be useless. They inspired me, though, to help my students (and myself) to develop an appreciation for more than the fire-hosed content often delivered in classrooms.

Think about the great people of the world—those who made a difference, a significant impact. Chances are they excelled in one or more of the above areas. Nelson Mandela, Abraham Lincoln, Rosa Parks, Gandhi, Martin Luther King, Jr., Samuel Adams, Frederick Douglass, Elie Wiesel, Maya Angelou, and Mother Teresa come to mind.

These skills separate the cogs from the linchpins. They demarcate those who *settle* from those who strive toward a dream and those who play it safe from those who fail fast and forward.

Gandhi reportedly implored us to "be the change you wish to see in the world."

Indeed.

Consideration, Conversation, & Collaboration

❧

* Which of the six values above do you see regularly in your community? How has it helped your community grow—and how can it continue to help you grow?
* For the coming week, challenge yourself and someone you care about to take specific action and develop one of the six values above. Next week, work on a different one. And repeat. Think of the change you can generate.
* Which of the above values do you not see regularly in your community—and would like to see as part of the community fabric? How could it help your community members grow?
* What other questions do you need to address regarding this topic?

Procrastination[120]

❧

You know Ida Only, don't you? I'm sure you, like me, have spent some time with her. And when we do, it generally leads to regret, second guessing, teeth-gnashing, angst, and stress.

If you have been spending time with Ida, I suggest you end your relationship immediately. Otherwise she will own you.

I know a lot of people who have spent time with her. Ida really gets around! Like the students who failed a course. You might hear them say:

* If *Ida Only* spent more time studying, I wouldn't be on academic probation.

The employee who did not prepare adequately for her major presentation to the perspective client:

* If *Ida Only* done my preparation, I would have landed that account.

Perhaps you have heard you or others say:

* If *Ida Only* saved more, I could have retired by now.
* If *Ida Only* called a taxi, I wouldn't have that DUI.
* If *Ida Only* paid attention to my diet and exercise, I would not be 20 pounds overweight.

- If *Ida Only* paid more attention to my partner, kids, friends, community....
- If *Ida Only* said....
- If *Ida Only* done....
- If *Ida Only* known ....

Ida Only, indeed. A relationship with *Ida Only* has no future—other than one of contrition, remorse, disappointment, and heartbreak.

Why not make this week the beginning of a new relationship with *Ida's* sister, *Imma?*

Imma Only going to do what moves my life in healthy, ethical, and courageous directions. *Imma Only* going to live a life of integrity and passion.

What's your first step? Who will it be with–*Ida* or *Imma?*

Consideration, Conversation, & Collaboration

❦

* What excuses seem to be hindering your community?
* Why do these excuses exist? Fear? Laziness? Lack of leadership? Absence of time or money? Lack of training?
* What impact do these excuses have on your community?
* Now that you have awareness about the *what* and the *why* of these excuses, what actions will you take to eliminate them?
* What other questions do you need to address regarding this topic?

Negotiable or Non-Negotiable[121]

⟨≈⟩

TIME MANAGEMENT IS A MYTH. Can't be done. You can manage your finances (spend less, earn more). You can manage your weight (eat less, exercise more). You can even manage your stress level (rant less, breathe more). But you cannot manage time. You cannot get more of it. You cannot save some from this week and use it next week. Nope, you can't. You have 168 hours in every week. You cannot rearrange them.

What you can do is *manage your priorities*. That is something we all can do. Those little choices we make each day are a window to our priorities.

My students used to complete an activity titled "Where Does Your Week Go?" It consisted of a simple listing of what they did each hour of each day for a week. They then ranked each activity from *not necessary* to *extremely necessary*.

Necessary in this context means "does the stuff you fill your life with connect to your priorities?" In short, does the *stuff you do* get you closer to what you identify as your goals? Doing a lot of stuff is NOT the same as doing the *right* stuff.

Another way to look at this is to determine whether your activities are negotiable or non-negotiable.

For a single parent, the care of his or her child is non-negotiable. Likewise, your physical health is non-negotiable. Three hours spent on social media each day may fall in the negotiable category.

Look at your list of activities for this week. Do they rank as negotiable or non-negotiable? Are you doing the right things or are you just doing stuff?

A money budget can help you determine where your money comes from and where it goes. It can be a tedious process—but it is a necessary exercise for building wealth. The same with a time budget. Keeping track of everything you do for 168 hours will provide insights about how you use your time.

This week focus on your necessary (non-negotiable) priorities, minimize the unnecessary (negotiable) activities, and activate positive new habits.

Consideration, Conversation, & Collaboration

- For the next seven days, keep a log of how you use your time. Record your sleep, your meals, your social media use, exercise, and time spent with your kids, spouse, and friends. Record everything. And remember, the total number of hours MUST add up to 168 hours. Exactly. Once you have completed the log, judge the nature of each hour in your week on a scale from 1 (not necessary) to 5 (extremely necessary). And then answer for yourself: Am I doing the right things, or am I just doing stuff?

- One of my most-watched YouTube videos, "Priority Management: Are You Doing the Right Things or Are You Just Doing Stuff?"[122] demonstrates a memorable visual I created for my students about what happens when we get sidetracked in life and fill our days with the small stuff—the negotiable items.

    A note about the video. It is in three parts: (1) the setup, (2) the problem, and (3) the conclusion and lesson. Listen to the great observations and thoughts from the students participating in this video with me. Classroom teachers and workshop facilitators who may be reading this: Consider this as one way to introduce and/or reinforce the concept of priority management. You could show it in three segments; pause the video after each segment; have the students write a reflection; then conclude with a group discussion. Have fun with it!

- How can you connect the above demonstration to community development?

- What other questions do you need to address regarding this topic?

A Post-Fact World[123]

❧

Have we morphed into a post-fact world?

Information literacy focuses on four steps:

1. Identify what pertinent information is needed to complete a task;
2. Understand where to find the facts related to the issue;
3. Evaluate the information for soundness, accuracy, and currency; and
4. Organize and use the information for a cogent and honest presentation.

These criteria are used to represent a straight-forward teaching approach. Today, it has become more difficult to hold conversations about controversial topics. Camps of opinion, which are not new, become bitterly hostile. Anything, true or not, that does not connect to a person's beliefs is not only subject to disagreement, it better brace itself for virulent personal rants and attacks.

I always encouraged vigorous debate in my classrooms. All sides welcomed, if three things were present:

1. Civility and respect;
2. A clearly stated fact, proposition, or thesis; and
3. Support (read: facts) to buttress the proposition or thesis.

While some students fell back on the old canard, "If-it's-my-opinion-it-can't-be-wrong" argument, most made the effort to present evidence.

Have we moved to a place where instead of *truth* we settle for *truthiness*? Can the *facts* be replaced with *alternative facts*? And who become the *fact checkers*?

How do you understand information literacy in a social media culture where millions yell for attention each day?

Do you remember the question, "If a tree falls in the forest and no one hears it, did it make a sound?"

Perhaps we live in a time when the question to ponder has become, "If a fact is offered and it is not *liked,* is it a fact?"

Consideration, Conversation, & Collaboration

❦

- In what ways do your communities work to ensure responsible conversations about issues that matter? Is *fake news* an issue for your members? If so, how?
- What *weak signals* have presented themselves in your communities concerning facts, truth, opinion, fiction, and lies? What steps can you take (have you taken) to capitalize on these weak signals? Is this an issue within your communities?
- Consider having a facilitated conversation about what true communication looks and sounds like.
- What other questions do you need to address regarding this topic?

A Deeper Dive: VPEER

For this exercise, focus on two communities of which you are a member. One should be a vibrant and prospering community. The other ranks amongst the weakest. Name each one below.

My strongest community is _____.

My weakest community is _____.

Now, for each community answer the questions below.

- **Visualize** the purpose, journey, and membership of your community. What *weak signals* exist to indicate the future of your community will not look like the past? What does this future focus tell you? What does the community you envision look like?
- **Prioritize** the resources you will need, and the actions required to sustain your community—and make it thrive into the future. What non-negotiable steps do you need to take? What comes first? How will you prioritize the value of **RESPONSIBILITY** to help build and strengthen your community? Who needs to do what?
- **Exorcise** that which no longer serves or nourishes your community. How can you minimize or eliminate the pernicious effects? Where does this fit with your prioritization of resources and actions? Who will help you identify these factors? Where will this fit in your prioritization?
- **Exercise** and strengthen the emotional, physical, and spiritual dimensions of life. Community building can be challenging work. How will you and your members build and maintain a healthy lifestyle moving forward? Where can you find this on your list of priorities?

- **Realize** your visualization. How often will you stop to evaluate your progress? How will you realize if you are faithfully following the four steps above (visualize, prioritize, exorcise, and exercise)?

Reflection

*Taking time to consider, ponder, remember, analyze, evaluate,
and appreciate the various connections of life.*

⚛

RELATED TERMS INCLUDE: ASSUMPTIONS, CHOICES, *accountability, communication,
creativity, goals, inspiration, present moment, mindful, and vulnerability.*[124]

A TRANSFORMATIONAL STORY ABOUT COMMUNITY: "BE THE GROWN-UP IN THE ROOM"

This section-opener differs from others in the book. Those stories high-light a specific program, neighborhood, or organization. This one looks to a key resource for each of those entities—the leaders.

Transformation does not just appear. It requires vision, thought, communication, respect, difficult questioning, and attentive listening. Transformational leaders help orchestrate that communal dance. They recognize that establishing a *shared vision* requires tough conversations. Everyone around the table typically sees his or her agenda item as the most important. They struggle to understand what *community* means beyond their narrow framework. *Intentions* may be good, but *attention* may not stray far from an individual agenda. The bigger picture can get lost in collective monologues.

One day in the gym, my personal trainer posed a question I've mentioned in a previous chapter about mind-body discipline and fitness:

"How do people walk around in something they were born with and not know anything about it or not be aware of what affects it?"

The same can be said for community leadership: "How do you lead a community if you do not take time to understand what affects it? How do you *live* or *work* in *a place* and not know anything about it or not be aware of what affects it?"

Two long-time community activists and leaders shared a few leadership skills and strategies with me on a mid-summer visit to their home.[125] When I sat down with Linda and Michael Lanier, I wanted to learn how leaders get people to engage in reflective practice. How do they get the people at the table to pause, consider, converse, and collaborate?

Linda Lanier's storied leadership career included having served as the head of the Jacksonville, Florida, affiliate of the Planned Parenthood Federation of America, the Executive Director of the Sulzbacher Center for the Homeless, and head of the Jacksonville Children's Commission. She said effective leaders understand that they must say what everybody knows but few want to own. The leader sets the tone by "speaking truth to power and saying the unspeakable."

That is, the leader must provide the safe, yet possibly uncomfortable, means for an open and honest discussion about tough issues.

Michael, a former behavioral therapist and recently retired as a hospital vice president for community outreach, said the leader needs to help his team move beyond passivity, navigate through emotion and upset, and be real by explaining the situation. He must help the parties at the table see a higher sense. They must keep their calling in mind.

"In the hospital," he said, "I always went back to our mission. We had to help those whose lives had been interrupted by illness or injury." He always kept that mission front and center for his staff and himself.

Michael and Linda believe that leaders need to tune into the vulnerabilities of the people sitting around the table. Ask them to help you (the leader) to understand the issue at hand by drawing on their wisdom.

Linda said effective leaders, "Draw out rather than pump in. They help people discover what they already know. And to do this, you have to start with assumptions—do not start with the solutions. Always remember that all of us are smarter than any one of us."

But what about the defenses and walls people bring to the table? Don't we have to deconstruct those before we build for the future?

"Those defenses present themselves for a reason," Michael said. "And we must respect them and be mindful not to trip on them as we move forward."

Linda was more direct, "Someone must be the grown-up in the room. The leader sets the tone."

How can a reflective leader help her team set the tone, especially in a highly charged conversation? How can she be the grown-up in the room? The Laniers's strategies include:

* Reflect on what you (the leader) will say. Provide insights with transparency and support;
* Work diligently to make sure the people in front of you believe they are seen and heard;
* Take risks. Reveal your concerns while avoiding a *know-it-all* demeanor. In fact, at the beginning of meetings, Michael often wrote a one-word reminder across the top of his copy of the agenda: *Humble*;
* Be realistic about your expectations; and
* Remember that kindness is always better than righteousness.

Finally, Linda shared that leaders need to move beyond *hope*. While hoping for a better outcome is laudable, it will come up short if the people you work with (team members as well as clients) have no reference point for the vision. The leader needs to help us see what is possible, especially when we do not have that vision in our experience.

Once that vision of what we desire comes into focus, we then need to hold a belief we can access that pathway—that we have the wherewithal to accomplish the envisioned goal. But, if cause and effect are broken, it becomes difficult to move forward. That can stymie any community.

Reflective leaders help place cause and effect in proper perspective. And then they guide their team forward with consideration, conversation, and collaboration.

Tough? You bet. Worth it? Definitely.

Before You Start

❦

CONSIDER COMMUNITIES TO WHICH YOU belong. How does **REFLECTION** help the vibrant ones prosper and the struggling ones grow?

For instance, think of a dynamic community to which you belong. In what ways does **REFLECTION** in that community contribute to its growth and resilience? Conversely, what do your struggling communities lack when it comes to **REFLECTION**?

Reflect on what the Laniers said about leadership. How do the leaders in your communities:

* Provide insights with transparency and support?
* Work to make sure the people are seen and heard?
* Take risks and reveal their concerns while avoiding a *know-it-all* demeanor?
* Remain realistic about expectations? and
* Believe and act like kindness is always better than righteousness?

Below you will find blog post excerpts related to the concept of **REFLECTION**. Choose one, read it, and consider its message. You will probably note that one or more of the other Seven Rs come into play as well. These core values mutually reinforce one another. Begin a conversation about how you and your community can use the points to foster and sustain community.

Then, repeat with the other blog excerpts.

After each excerpt you will find several suggestions and specific questions on how to bring the teachings of the piece to life in your community. Rather than settling for general answers, use the following three-step model to help you be more actionable with your responses.

1. Establish a realistic, feasible, time-bound plan for implementing your proposed actions.

2. Execute your plan. Make sure all involved understand their roles and responsibilities.
3. Evaluate your progress on a regular basis. Adjust course as needed.

Words for Reflection[126]

❧

QUOTES CAN BE POWERFUL REMINDERS and motivators. They, also, can become trite and meaningless if repeated like so many bumper stickers without reflection. Reflect on the five quotes below. After each one, I offer some reflections on those words.

- **I don't need a friend who changes when I change and who nods when I nod; my shadow does that much better.**—attributed to Plutarch
    - Do not surround yourself with *yes* people. We need honest people around us who will help us understand what we do well—and what we need to tweak or totally change. A senior school administrator from Massachusetts shared with me that the *yes* people of an organization do everyone a disservice. They will "lead you down the primrose path to destruction."
- **The best time to plant a tree is 20 years ago. The second-best time is now.**—attributed to Chinese Proverb
    - What are you waiting for? Today is the tomorrow you created yesterday.
- **Every system is perfectly designed to get the results it gets.**—Attribution disputed[127]
    - The results we get come from what we do, where we do it, whom we do it with (or choose not to do it with), and how we do it. Einstein said something like if we keep doing things

the same way but expect different results that is the definition of insanity. Speaking of Einstein....

* **Try not to become a man of success but a man of value.**—attributed to Albert Einstein

  * We can get so caught up in *doing something* and *being somebody*
  that we can lose sight of *why* we are doing what we are doing.
  Are we making a difference in the world? Do we add value to
  the lives around us? I once read this advice. Rather than asking a new acquaintance, "What do you do for a living?" ask
  "What do you offer?" That will catch attention! What do *you*
  offer? What do *I* offer?

* **When loved ones come home, always run to greet them.**—Ilan
Shamir (From "Advice from a Dog")

  * Our dog, Roxie, lives these words. Each day, each moment, is
  full of wonder. Whatever the day may bring, greet your loved
  ones with open arms, a smile, and a kind word. Heck, really
  shake them up and wag your tail a couple of times! It is pretty
  simple. Woof!

Consideration, Conversation, & Collaboration

Apply each of the above quotes to your community.

* **I don't need a friend who changes when I change and who nods when I nod; my shadow does that much better.**
    * Who asks the authentic, yet difficult, questions your community needs to hear and grapple with to grow?
    * Who can help the community members ask deeper questions for their growth and resilience?
* **The best time to plant a tree is 20 years ago. The second-best time is now.**
    * What has your community been putting off that needs attention now?
    * What have you been putting off that needs attention now?
* **Every system is perfectly designed to get the results it gets.**
    * In what ways is your community "perfectly designed to get" what it gets? How is this a positive? How is this not-so positive?
* **Try not to become a man of success but a man of value.**
    * In what ways does your community make a positive difference in the lives of its members? What weak signals exist that may indicate a transformation is needed?
* **When loved ones come home, always run to greet them.**
    * What does your community do to make members feel at home and welcomed in their neighborhoods?
    * How does this extend to visitors and non-community members?
* What other questions do you need to address regarding this topic?

REFLECTION 6.2
Embrace Now[128]

☙

ONE MEDITATION SESSION I PARTICIPATED in centered on the simple words, "Now is my time!" Wherever we find ourselves, no matter the situation, recognize this is where we need to be currently. Embrace it. Grow with it. The *now* is what we have in hand.

It reminds us that constantly focusing on the result will cause us to miss the journey. Speaking as someone who is very goal-driven, I realize I spend far too much of my life either focused on what I have no control over (the past) or that which has yet to transpire (the future). When I spend time in the past and in the future, I miss the present. I miss what is *with* me—and will soon become the past. And when I ruminate on making the future better—again I miss the present. Do you see the endless self-defeating cycle? Our choices have brought us to our current state.

Now is truly all we are sure of at any time. What are we doing with the *now* we are experiencing?

One semester, as we approached finals week on campus, I wanted to help my students celebrate what they had accomplished for the semester (past), what was ahead of them (future), but more importantly, I wanted them to remember that what they become today (present) will move them along their journey.

I sent the following email to my students. Maybe there is a nugget of inspiration for you and your community.

Good morning, young scholars!

You have arrived into the homestretch of the semester. Now, you can see what you have accomplished. Congratulate yourself. And get ready to cross the finish line with style and grace.

Here is a quick strategy to keep your energy and passion flowing. Repeat the following out loud: "Now is MY time!" Say it again. "Now is MY time!"

Yes, you may have lots of responsibilities with family, children, work, and school. You must always take care of the NON-NEGOTIABLE priorities in your life.

And at times you might feel like quitting and walking away from your education. Remember that each day brings you closer to your dreams—but only if YOU continue to move toward your dreams. This is your time. What will you do with it?

I look forward to a wonderfully energizing end of the semester with you. And remember to say—and mean it—and be it: "Now is MY time!"

As you prepare for your week ahead, embrace today. Tomorrow, today will be yesterday. *Now* really is the time. How will you embrace and nurture it?

Consideration, Conversation, & Collaboration

∽∾

* Often, we can miss the *now* in our community. We leave for work before daylight, return after the sun sets. Drive into the garage, close the door, have dinner with the family, help the kids with homework, and check our emails. Who has time for the community? It will be there tomorrow (the future) we think. What can you do to embrace the *now* of your community, today (the present)?

* How often do you and your neighbors reflect on and celebrate the beauty of what exists in your community? How can you do more of this?

* What have been activities or events that have brought your community members together to share and enjoy each other's company? Consider things like pot-luck dinners, trivia nights, backyard barbecues, front porch gatherings, birthday parties, neighborhood cleanups, book clubs, or faith-based meetings.

* What other questions do you need to address regarding this topic?

Set Your Agenda[129]

❦

EVERY CARDIO MACHINE IN OUR local gym has the ubiquitous television monitor attached to it. And every morning you will find members dutifully burning off calories, building stamina, and getting their daily agenda, in part or in full, set for them.

Maybe you know people for whom, after awakening each morning, the first exercise they get is to grab the remote or tablet and check the morning *news alerts*. Perhaps they had fallen asleep the night before with the last thing they heard coming from the agenda of someone else's mouth.

A study[130] from more than 40 years ago found

> *In choosing and displaying news, editors, newsroom staff, and broadcasters play an important part in shaping political reality. Readers learn not only about a given issue, but also how much importance to attach to that issue from the amount of information in a news story and its position....*

According to dictionary.com, *news* is defined as "the presentation of a report on recent or new events in a newspaper or other periodical or on radio or television."

We should address whether the news is really *news*. Other than a change in name or location, for instance, does the general presentation of the news change?

Look at most programming and you have some semblance of this order: "Breaking News Alert" followed by "story about death" followed by "story about destruction" followed by "story about weather catastrophe" followed by "story about crash during rush hour" followed by "story about economic calamity" followed by....

Doesn't really sound *newsy* to me.

It would be simplistic to state that the news tells us how to think. It may not be much of a stretch, however, to say that the news does direct what we think about if we allow it.[131] And it's not just the network or cable news. If I were to wake up and immediately go to my social media feed, I stand the chance of my *friends* setting my agenda for the day.

Perhaps you have heard it said that you are the *average* of the people with whom you spend most of your time. This view believes who we hang with matters in terms of physical health, emotional outlook, expectations for the future, and acceptance of others. These fellow-travelers can, if we let them, set our agenda for the day. Give yourself some time to think, reflect, set YOUR course, and then invite them onto YOUR agenda.

Years ago, I decided that I would take more control of setting my daily agenda. Not just the to-do list, but my mindset as well. I don't wish to start my day with someone squawking at me from the TV or screaming through my earbuds. I seldom read the newspaper with my morning coffee. I will have time enough to get to my email. I am fortunate to live in a loving relationship that starts the day with pleasantries rather than an argument.

I have eliminated just about all news alerts on my devices. Among the few exceptions: baseball, local weather, and airline texts when I travel. Why let someone else interrupt my thought process and mindset with what they see as something I *need* to know *right now* from the *world out there?*

Yes, of course, when an emergency arises, I can tune in. But if every moment of every day is an *emergency* then we might need to redefine *emergency.*

Even if your start time is only 15 or 30 minutes (or five or ten minutes) before the world starts calling you, why not take control of that little time to set your intentions for the day? Their attention-seeking messages will come calling soon enough.

Consideration, Conversation, & Collaboration

- Who sets the agenda for your community? Why is this the case? How is this working?
- Consider a technology-free dinner. Everyone must place their cell phones and tablets in a secure, out-of-sight location. They cannot access them until the evening event has completed. They will need to engage in face-to-face conversation.
- What other questions do you need to address regarding this topic?

A Bit Off-Center[132]

❧

I DABBLE WITH PHOTOGRAPHY. WHETHER my 35mm camera, smartphone, or the action unit mounted to my kayak, I have fun, get creative, learn, and further appreciate the environment around me.

A shutterbug friend tutored me about shooting a scene off-center. That is, placing the focal point of the shot to the left or right. Such a view creates a more dynamic presentation. It helps move the eye and create interest.

Before this advice, I shot most of my photos, interestingly, with the subject dead center in the frame. The colors and textures created interest, but after a few shots, I could see what she meant. There seemed to be a sameness. Something was missing.

As I played with the angles and perspectives, I had an *aha moment*. By shifting the focus, a little this way or that, the entire scene took on a renewed perspective.

This got me thinking about how we can view our community. While a centered focus helps us zero in on the big part of the picture like a goal, we might miss those things just off to the side. Maybe these items provide color or a bit more texture. This additional information can be useful in understanding and appreciating the larger glory and story. By going a little off-center, we start to see things that can enhance our view. We open ourselves up to larger possibilities and opportunities.

Consideration, Conversation, & Collaboration

❧

- Where can you shift your focus to see a problem, an opportunity, or a major community decision from a different perspective? What little things might you be missing because you will not move the focal point? A little this way; a little that way. A bit more texture; a different hue. A clearer view. More mindful.
- On what can you adjust your focus this week? Where can you go a bit off-center for a different—and perhaps—renewed perspective?
- What other questions do you need to address regarding this topic?

Ask. Listen. Act.[133]

❧

I STOOD IN THE BACK of an auditorium in New Mexico. In ten minutes, I would be introduced to an audience of about 1,000 public school teachers. They had come to hear me for their mandatory professional development day.

One of the organizers leaned over and whispered in my ear. "You got a big group today! And, about 900 of them don't want to be here." He smiled.

Thanks!

One summer afternoon I facilitated a four-hour workshop for 80 community college faculty. The organizer told me that the event was mandatory for the faculty.

One would hope the people forced to attend *training* would have input into what the program would cover. In my experience, that rarely happens.

I noticed a similar dynamic at a community meeting. Knowledgeable, civil, compassionate, and respectful people sat around the table with thoughts, plans, and initiatives for what we could do for our community. Great ideas of how to help people and improve well-being. What was not part of the initial comments was the question, "Have we asked the people (our neighbors) what they want or need?" Simple. Yet often overlooked in the hurry to do what we *know* is the right thing to do.

Noise abounds as people will gladly tell us what we should or should not do. Perhaps we do the same to others. (Probably do!) At times, we go for the quick answer or what we think is the resolution and miss the eloquence of pertinent questions.

Ask authentic and meaningful questions. Listen and ask more questions. Then act with purpose, direction, and collaboration.

Consideration, Conversation, & Collaboration

- Consider the latest initiative in your community. It could deal with parks, streets, noise, development, police presence, schools, or flood control. Who had authentic and meaningful input before the initiative was announced? Who did not? How do you account for this?

- One author and business consultant[134] lays out a simple premise, "If you're not happy with the current state of your company, you have three choices. You can live with it, leave it, or change it." Pick one dimension that needs some tweaking—that needs change. Then ask yourself a few beginning questions.
  - What happens if we live with the current state of dis-ease? What will that look like?
  - What happens if we leave the current state of dis-ease? How will we do that and what will that look like?
  - What happens if we change the current state of dis-ease? How will we do that and what will that look like?

- Change can be messy. Change can be healthy. Change can take time. Meaningful change requires that we raise our *awareness*, question our *assumptions*, and take considered *action*. How does your community address each of these three As?

- I dug back into my video archives for "Feeding Your Mind. Creating Your Life."[135] Although I recorded this on the last day of 2011, the message remains: What do we choose to allow into our lives? What do you have power to change?

- What other questions do you need to address regarding this topic?

Past. Present. Future.[136]

❧

BEYOND ACADEMIC ACHIEVEMENT, TEACHERS DO well to help students honor their past, celebrate their present, and look to their future. [137]

Honor the Past. The past has been the vehicle that has carried us to this moment. I encourage my students to understand and respect their past. Sure, there are moments, events, people, and issues that may be troubling at best and traumatic at worst. *Honoring* in this context means to recognize that from those times, you have grown into the person you are. It does not diminish what happened. The past should not be an excuse—nor should it be a shackle. It happened; it cannot be undone.

I have watched organizational managers state they were not responsible for the past they inherited. They would not be bogged down in memories. While these new folks did not create the history of the organization, they created a new history. And to not understand and respect what their organization has gone through—the culture that their followers have experienced—is short-sighted and disrespectful. Never forget or disrespect the institutional memory (the community history) as you move the organization forward.

Celebrate the Present. The present is all we have. While there is wisdom in preparing for the future, we can get lost in it and miss what we are truly experiencing. The present is our time to live and create our evolving history. When we hold on to the past, going beyond honoring to becoming *stuck in the past*, it robs us of our present. When we live in the future, we vacate the present. Once gone, we cannot get the present back.

Embrace the Future. For some, the future is scary. For others, that unknown is cause for excitement rather than trepidation. There is a practicality in looking to the future. For example, retirement planning for the future takes place in the present. Today is the tomorrow you prepared for (or not) yesterday.

Students enter college with their dreams. In many ways, those who have the privilege to work in the classroom help coach these folks to their future. Inspirational and far-sighted leaders have a responsibility to focus on the future.

Existentialist Soren Kierkegaard receives credit for reminding us that "Life can only be understood backwards; but it must be lived forwards." Leaders help people reflect, respect, and reach.

Consideration, Conversation, & Collaboration

❧

- Honor the Past. What do you see as a defining moment in your community's history? In what way did it help the community to grow? What insights did the community gain?
- Celebrate the Present. What defining moment presents itself for your community today?
- Embrace the Future. Are there any weak signals in the present that may indicate what the future holds for your community?
- What other questions do you need to address regarding this topic?

Choose Advisors Carefully[138]

CORPORATIONS HAVE BOARDS OF DIRECTORS. Institutions of higher learning and non-profit organizations have Boards of Trustees to provide oversight and guidance. They may be made up of passionate people who are deeply committed to the mission of the operation they advise. Some may be very active; and others mere window dressing acting as rubber stamps for the organization's leaders.

Do you have your own Board of Directors (BOD)?

Perhaps you already have a mentor, a coach, or a group of people who can advise you on various aspects of your career—and your life.

I have taken the notion of a BOD seriously. I have recruited those who can offer guidance, direction, and pointed questions. Below you will find a few of the *slots* I have filled. I am having fun with this while remaining focused on surrounding myself with knowledgeable and skillful people who will have my back and kick me in the butt when needed.

I have listed ten Board members you might want to consider for your own BOD.

1. CHAIR. This person is the choreographer of the Board. You need someone with vision and a depth of experience.
2. COO: Chief Outside Officer. It is easy to become myopic if we only look at our industry/business/calling from within those boundaries. Get someone with a fresh pair of eyes who may not know much about what you do, but who will be able to see opportunities or shortcomings you have long since overlooked.

3. CQO: Chief Questioning Officer. Get someone who knows how to—and is not afraid to—ask the tough questions. Instead of brainstorming, this person will lead you in *question-storming* on a regular basis. This person could double as your Chief Creative Thinker (CCT).

4. CMO: Chief Marketing/Messaging Officer. How will you market yourself, service, product, community, or cause? Find someone who has such experience. You need someone to help you get your message before the right people.

5. CCO: Chief Content Officer. Marketing (see above) won't help you if your product or service is garbage. Find someone who can help you with depth, research, and credibility.

6. CEO: Chief Entertainment Officer. Who will help you keep things light? Humor lightens the day and keeps us from taking ourselves too seriously. Who will mix things up for you and your *people?* Don't forget to have a little music in your day as well.

7. CLO: Chief Logistics Officer. This person can help with daily tasks and travel arrangements. If you are immersed in the tiny details of day-to-day operations, you may not have the time to develop your true talent. You may never be able to grow your talent into a true strength if you remain neck-deep in minutiae.

8. CWO: Chief Wellness Officer. Maintain your balance and well-being. If you don't already have an exercise and diet plan, this person can help jumpstart that part of your life. If you have one, your CWO will keep you on task.

9. CFO: Chief Financial Officer. Like it or not, we all need a bean counter or two in our lives. Not only for the day-to-day operations, but also for our long-term wealth building.

10. CO-NOBS: Chief Officer of No BS. Please do not surround yourself with *yes* people. You need folks who will constantly hold you accountable—and call BS when needed.

Make your board functional. It should move you forward in the service of your calling. It should help you develop your talent and skills. It should help you keep your passion stoked! What other slots would you create for your BOD?

Consider: Why stop with your business or professional side? Consider a family BOD as well. You might not be the Chair–but there are plenty of other positions for which you have a talent. Call an organizational meeting tonight!

Consideration, Conversation, & Collaboration

❦

* Maybe your community or neighborhood block does not need formal and structured board of advisors. Consider the titles above. How can you fit those functions into your community structure? For instance, who has a knack for pulling together social get-togethers? Maybe that person is your CEO. Who can get to the heart of matters with incisive questioning (CQO)? And so on....
* For a video presentation of the above, see "Do You Have Your Own Board of Directors?"[139]
* What other questions do you need to address regarding this topic?

A Deeper Dive: VPEER

For this exercise, focus on two communities with which you have membership. One should be a vibrant and prospering community. The other ranks amongst the weakest. Name each one below.

My strongest community is _____.

My weakest community is _____.

Now, for each community answer the questions below.

* **Visualize** the purpose, journey, and membership of your community. What *weak signals* exist to indicate the future of your community will not look like the past? What does this future focus tell you? What does the community you envision look like?
* **Prioritize** the resources you will need, and the actions required to sustain your community—and make it thrive into the future. What non-negotiable steps do you need to take? What comes first? How will you prioritize **REFLECTION** to help build and strengthen your community?
* **Exorcise** that which no longer serves or nourishes your community. How can you minimize or eliminate the pernicious effects? Where does this fit with your prioritization of resources and actions? Who will help you identify these factors? Where will this fit in your prioritization?
* **Exercise** and strengthen the emotional, physical, and spiritual dimensions of life. Community building can be challenging work. How will you and your members build and maintain a healthy lifestyle moving forward? Where can you find this on your list of priorities?

* **Realize** your visualization. How often will you stop to evaluate your progress? How will you realize if you are faithfully following the four steps above (visualize, prioritize, exorcise, and exercise)?

Resilience

The ability to connect adaptability, recovery, discovery, and growth.

⋘⬥⋙

RELATED TERMS INCLUDE: BALANCE, CHANGE, critical thinking, distractions, failure, fitness, gratitude, inspiration, integration, leadership, legacy, risk, and vulnerability.[140]

A TRANSFORMATIONAL STORY ABOUT COMMUNITY: "FACING THE WORST. PREPARING FOR THE BEST."

The concept of *relationships* opened this book. Section One showed how connections—people-to-people, face-to-face—help build a community. Section Three reminded us that resources are more than *things* and *services*. Relationships remain the secret sauce. Connected people create, nurture, and sustain the best resource a community has to offer.

As we move into our final section of the book, we will see how relationships play a pivotal role in establishing, bolstering, and sustaining resilience. That is the story from two Jacksonville, Florida, community activists who have been voices for countless women facing a breast cancer diagnosis. One as a survivor and one as an organizer for survivors.[141] Both became key community players helping people embrace their agency—their power to control their destinies.

Bobbi de Cordova-Hanks was enjoying life as a bass guitar player, magazine editor, and newlywed, when she got the news in 1986 that she had breast cancer. Though as she relates in the book she and her husband wrote, *Tears of Joy*,[142] the doctor seemed to use every word *but cancer.* Bobbi said, at the time, there was a stigma to the *C* word. The Big C. It seemed that to utter the word was the same as proclaiming a death sentence. No one wanted to talk about it.

Well, almost no one. Bobbi did in 1988 when she formed the support group *Bosom Buddies.* Likewise, a woman very much in the public eye, created another pathway for agency.

Jeannie Blaylock, co-anchor of the evening news for First Coast News (Channel 12) in Jacksonville, Florida, was not a cancer survivor. Nor was she living with a diagnosis. She was grappling, however, with the sudden and tragic death of her 29-year-old friend to breast cancer. In 1993, Jeannie used her visibility as a news reporter to shed light on the topic. She initiated *Buddy Check 12*, encouraging women to connect and remind one another, on the 12th of each month, to conduct a breast self-exam. With her persistence, the station aired segments showing actual models conducting breast exams in the shower, lying down, and sitting up. This was unheard of for the time and market. And most definitely needed. The first night, the station received 234 calls from women. A door had been opened.

Jeannie remembers speaking with a woman, who in hushed tones on the phone, said she did not know how to tell her husband. She feared he would divorce her. While speaking the women hurriedly hung up saying, "Oh, no, he just came home. I have to go."

Meanwhile by 1993, Bobbi was formally a *survivor* and her *Bosom Buddies* steadily gained momentum. Starting with just three women in the initial support group, the organization had served more than 7,000 by 2018.

I asked Bobbi, "How did you survive the diagnosis, the treatment, and at least at the time (1980s), the social and workplace stigma of breast cancer?"

The first thing she had to do was recognize the situation was bigger than herself, bigger than anything she had ever tackled in her life.

She prayed. "When I was given a death sentence, I had to go to someone upstairs."

She, also, found humor in an otherwise dark situation. "I told myself that I was too busy to die. And, after all, no other woman can wear my jewelry!"

She asked her doctors hard questions and demanded clear and pointed answers. She stood up for herself and her husband. When patients are diagnosed with cancer, Bobbi said, "Everyone around them has also been diagnosed with cancer." That includes the caregivers. It's a community. She had something greater than herself to live for.

She came to understand the importance of the mind/body connection and of the difference that emotional support can make to newly diagnosed women. In her book, she shared that she "desperately needed other women to talk to, especially those who had been diagnosed with breast cancer and lived to talk about it. I felt like cancer was a death sentence. Now I know it's a life sentence." She came to focus on seven words: "Facing the worst. Preparing for the best."

Bosom Buddies gave women a forum to share stories and learn from the survivors. "What? You too? I thought I was the only one," summed up the feeling when they learned they were not alone on this journey. No stigma involved. Friendships were born, and they helped grow resilience.

Like Bobbi's experience, Jeannie Blaylock found that no one wanted to talk about cancer. *Buddy Check 12* gave *permission*. Once the conversation started, no one was going to stop it. The women, she said, "had—and have—guts, spunk." In hearing other people's stories, they began to hear the "echo of a voice" of their story. They would not be denied and would not give up. Cancer was not about what could not be done. It was about what they would do.

Buddy Check 12 has become a national, intergenerational, and international movement. This growing breast cancer education and support program has developed legs over a quarter of a century. These are people, according to Jeannie, who are "staying alive for themselves and for the people they love."

Bobbi says that she and the thousands she has worked with remain proud to be survivors. They are victors, not victims.

"It's beyond surviving. It's thriving," she told me. "While a little humor goes a long way when you're wearing a prosthesis the size of a 38 double D, I needed more." She made a choice to connect with a support group. "That connection made me feel alive again," she said. "What a wonderful feeling...."

Relationships. That matter. Resilience.

Before You Start

❧

Consider communities to which you belong. How can the concept of **RESILIENCE** help the vibrant ones prosper and the struggling ones grow?

For instance, think of a dynamic community to which you belong. In what ways does your community contribute to its own growth and **RESILIENCE?** Conversely, what do your struggling communities lack when it comes to **RESILIENCE?** What kind of support (emotional, physical, spiritual, or financial) is available in challenging situations? Do your communities provide opportunities to have difficult conversations about difficult topics as a way to heal and grow?

Below you will find blog post excerpts related to the concept of **RESILIENCE.** Choose one, read it, and consider its message. You will probably note that one or more of the other Seven Rs come into play as well. These core values mutually reinforce one another. Begin a conversation about how you and your community can use the points to foster and sustain community.

Then, repeat with the other blog excerpts.

After each excerpt you will find several suggestions and specific questions on how to bring the teachings of the piece to life in your community. Rather than settling for general answers, use the following three-step model to help you be more actionable with your responses.

1. Establish a realistic, feasible, time-bound plan for implementing your proposed actions.
2. Execute your plan. Make sure all involved understand their roles and responsibilities.
3. Evaluate your progress on a regular basis. Adjust course as needed.

A Few Thoughts And Questions About Resilience[143]

❦

AS WE AGE, DO WE become more of ourselves? Do we become more of what we have already been in our lives? Like loving, fearful, cheerful, optimistic, pessimistic, healthy, kind, or mean based on our track record?

Can we become more resilient? Can we develop resilience only as a result of—maybe especially because of—difficult and horrific situations.

Or has resilience become a defined quality and quantity based on our background? Our DNA?

Do a quick search of the word *resilience* and you will find 66+ million internet hits, thousands of products on Amazon, and about three-quarters of a million YouTube videos.

The typical definition of resilience points to one's ability to rise above, recover from, move on from, and learn from adversity. But is that the only way one grows resilience? Do you see resilience as springing solely from adversity? Can it build from positive interactions in times that *lack* trauma?

Let's look at resilience from a slightly different perspective. Maybe we can approach resilience as a condition of being adaptable to a disaster and, also, living and sustaining a healthy life that avoids or at least, prepares for disaster before it happens.

Psychologist Edith Grotberg[144] believes we can develop resilience by focusing on three areas:

* What I Have (our support system of relationships);
* What I Am (our thoughts about others and ourselves); and
* What I Can (our ability to communicate and solve problems).

An adult friend related a traumatic experience he encountered as an adolescent. He is not sure how, but he not only rebounded from the incident, he thrived and developed critical survival strategies.

A mother shared with me the trials and tribulations of her teenaged son who was making ill-advised choices. She and her husband provided the support system *(tough love)* that helps (albeit slowly) the child grow his interpersonal and critical thinking skills. The parents continue to focus on the long game. When he comes out on the other end of this turbulent time, he will have developed coping mechanisms that will allow him to flourish. At least that is the hope.

Will he become more of what he has been or more of what he has the capacity to build within himself and for others? His strong support system points to the latter.

Consideration, Conversation, & Collaboration

✧

* How does your personal support system help you flourish in your life?
* How can you help someone develop or recognize their resilience this week?
* What support systems exist in your community that help members cope with and, eventually, flourish in tough situations and grow in others?
* What weak signals point to future community needs that may challenge underlying assumptions about resilience?
* What other questions do you need to address regarding this topic?

HTRB As Needed[145]

ONE DAY, A WOUNDED WARRIOR student in one of my classes had a particularly challenging morning. She felt herself about to lose emotional control. Rather than lash out or have a meltdown on campus, she stopped herself, turned around, and walked away from the latest of a long line of stressors. She found a quiet spot, sat down, and then, as she told me, "I hit the reset button."

After a few reflective moments, she collected her thoughts and made her way to class to face the day with a smile on her face.

I thought about those times when the world felt like a crushing boulder sitting on my chest. More times than I would like to remember, I let emotion take over in those situations. When I reacted rather than responded to a stressor, the result was ALWAYS less than optimal. I have wished I, too, had hit the reset button.

Stop. Be. Reset.

Here are a few examples of when that reset button can come in handy. As you read, consider your life and when it would be wise to hit the reset button (**HTRB).**

* Feeling overwhelmed by the day-after-day onslaught of grim economic, political, social, or climatological news?
    * **HTRB** —Put yourself on a *news fast.* Limit your intake and set your agenda, rather than letting others set your mindset for the day.

* Drained by energy vampires?
  * **HTRB** —Walk away when possible. Identify toxic relation-ships—and minimize or eliminate exposure. Set boundar-ies. Know your limits.
* Working too many hours?
  * **HTRB** —Understand why you are doing this? If the overtime is self-imposed, understand why you put yourself (and your loved ones) through a hellish schedule. Where can you make changes? What is truly valuable—your time, your health, or money? It's your call.
* Bored with routine?
  * **HTRB**—As best you can, stir things up! Sleep on the oppo-site side of the bed. Find a new route to drive to work. Do a different routine at the gym. Rearrange your work space or work duties. Volunteer in your community.
* Taking people around you for granted?
  * **HTRB**—Just stop it! These are the folks who sustain you. Make time for them.
* Feel like you are a failure and that life is overwhelming?
  * **HTRB**—Ask those who know you to tell you what they LOVE about you. Pay attention to the small yet wondrous things around you each day. Identify things and people for which you have gratitude.

There are no guarantees. **HTRB** is no cure-all. But what is the alterna-tive? I think it was Wayne Dyer[146] who suggested that, when we feel pain, we would do well to stop and remind ourselves that we can have this pain, or we can have peace. **HTRB** will not only get you moving in a positive direction, it will have a beneficial effect on those around you. They will be able to enjoy you for the gifts you have to offer each day.

Consideration, Conversation, & Collaboration

⚮

- When do you **HTRB**? What do you use as *go-to* strategies?
- Is there an issue that is dividing your community? Have positions and views become polarized? How can you begin with a small group of people to begin the process of **HTRB**? Refer to the **REFLECTION** chapter for additional strategies.
- How can you develop a community-based **HTRB** practice?
- What other questions do you need to address regarding this topic?

On Being Responsibly Selfish[147]

❦

ONE NEW YEAR'S DAY, MY wife and I joined several friends in a polar plunge into the Atlantic Ocean. Full disclosure: We live in Florida. *Polar* is used advisedly. We all posed for *before* photos and videos, ran into the water, and then posed for the *after* photos. Lots of fun. Refreshing. A good time!

Later that evening, when I reviewed the photos, there I stood in my bathing suit and New York Yankees ball cap. The suit and cap looked fine. Unfortunately, I cannot say the same for the ten extra pounds of Piscitelli hanging over my bathing suit waistline.

That photo was my wake-up call. It made me come face-to-face with the hard and uncomfortable fact that I had become complacent with my daily exercise regimen and eating habits.

That night—the first evening of the New Year—I made a commitment: I would become a better version of myself. Not for anybody else. I wanted this for me. I wanted to be a *more fit* me.

* I set a specific goal.
  * I would lose ten pounds before March 1 came up on the calendar.
* I set a specific plan.
  * I would pick up the pace, intensity, and duration during my 5:00 AM gym workouts. Nothing crazy. I just pushed myself

off the comfortable plateau on which I had been coasting along.
  * I would decrease my evening meal portion size.
* I acted.
  * Goals can quickly become fantasies if we do not act. So, I acted immediately.
* I saw results.
  * By the end of the 6th week (mid-February), I had not lost ten pounds. I had lost 12 pounds!
  * I had to have my pants altered. I had lost one and a half inches from my waist.
  * I had become a better version of me.

Do you have a vision of a better version of you? Maybe you want to shed a couple of pounds. Or perhaps you want to walk after dinner each night. Identify just ONE thing you can do now that will have a positive and healthy impact on your fitness level.

* Be smart. Set small specific goals on the way to the larger goals. You may need to consult your doctor or a certified fitness trainer for a plan that is matched to your needs and abilities.
  * What is your goal? What is that better version of you that you want to become?
* Do it. Act. Remember goals not acted on become fantasies.
  * When will you start?
* Be consistent. Do it again…and again. Make it a habit. Make it a lifestyle.
  * How often will you work toward your goals? What new habits do you have to create? What old habits do you have to stop?
* When it comes to your health be *responsibly selfish!* Treat yourself with respect. As one of my fitness trainers likes to say, "The worst thing that can happen is that you will get in shape."

Consideration, Conversation, & Collaboration

* One day I asked my fellow 5:00 AM gym travelers to share a few words of advice as to the HOWs and WHYs of their respective fitness regimens. In "Fitness: A Better Version of Me!"[148] you will notice a few repeating themes:
  * The process (the exercise) of staying fit makes them feel good.
  * Start your exercise routine by doing something you enjoy.
  * Start easy; start small; build from there. Small steps lead to big results.
  * Be consistent about your workout and your diet.
* Does your community have a community fitness goal? Do you have community fitness groups, like morning walking groups?
* What does a *better version our community* look like? How can you get to that vision?
* What other questions do you need to address regarding this topic?

Well-Being Is A Skillset[149]

⤬

IS IT POSSIBLE THAT YOUR workplace is killing you? Thought-provoking research published in the *Insights by Stanford Business*[150] examines that question. According to the report, workplace stressors include a lack of healthcare insurance, difficult work schedules, number of hours worked, work-life integration challenges, lack of social support, perceived or real workplace injustice, and lack of employment stability.

Just the perception of an unjust work environment can lead to 50 percent higher physician diagnosed illnesses. Fifty percent! Can you say, *toxic workplaces?* Look at the Stanford report and draw your conclusions.

It makes little difference what giveaways might be on the table at the company wellness fair or open enrollment meeting for healthcare plans. If the above stressors exist in your workplace, the research predicts dismal consequences. If words don't match actions, we end up with stories we tell vs. the stories we live. Disconnections abound.

If your workplace has a wellness initiative, is the focus too narrow? According to the paper "Creating an Engaged Culture through Wellbeing" from *Virgin Pulse*,[151] wellness programs need to focus on more than physical health (diet, weight, and exercise, for instance). Other dimensions of health exist and need to be in the mix. Rather than what can become a one-dimensional wellness initiative, focus on a more multi-dimensional concept of well-being.

In 2008, Pearson Education published and released my book *Rhythms of College Success*. I used the image of a six-string guitar as a metaphor for balance and well-being. Each string represented one of six dimensions of life. My description, in part, read:

> ...Visualize a six-string guitar. The guitar will be able to make sweet music with properly tuned strings. If one of the six strings falls out of tune or breaks, the guitar can still be played but the song will not be as pleasing.[152]

The farsighted work environment pays attention to the interplay of these multiple dimensions and to the significance of both individual habits and organizational culture. Reference the workplace stressors listed above.

Well-being, also, goes beyond the oft-cited goal of *work-life balance*. What I have been hearing and reading emphasizes *work-life integration or blend*. Work, after all, is a part of life. The concept of *integration* allows for more emphasis on flexibility of when we work, play, and create family time. And with flexibility comes responsibility. This requires the skill to set boundaries and limits so that the integration is a healthy blend.

Organizations may wish to examine the dynamic of work-life integration and place it within their well-being programs. Well-being does not just happen. It requires thought, planning, and follow-through. Management practices need to foster this sense of well-being. Leadership needs to model behavior such as providing clear and appropriate feedback, autonomy within one's job sphere and encouragement to set challenging and clearly articulated goals.

And leadership (true and caring leadership) needs to pay attention to the workplace stressors that may undermine individual well-being.

Consideration, Conversation, & Collaboration

❧

* What well-being activities does your community sponsor? How did it come to sponsor these events? How did it know these were what the community members wanted or needed? What else can be done?
* What resources does your community need to further develop its well-being activities? Consider a neighbor meet-and-greet to discuss resilience strategies for the coming year.
* What other questions do you need to address regarding this topic?

A Resilience Plan[153]

❦

NEARLY NINE MILLION SOULS WHO lost jobs during the Great Recession became part of the gig economy where they coble together multiple jobs (gigs) to pay the bills. Freelancing like this more than likely comes without paid vacation or sick leave.

And for those American workers who have vacation time as part of their salary package, many do not use—and many lose—the vacation time they earn each year. Due to overwork or fear or an inability to disconnect from the *labor-saving* devices, we have a growing number of American workers not taking *their time* to rejuvenate. And many who do take vacation, still work during their so-called time away. From emailing to texting, to working on documents, to phone calls, 61% of employed vacationers do some type of work during vacation (when they take it). [154]

Of course, you may hear the argument that when you love your job, well, it's not really work. You're just enhancing your vacation and better able to focus on your job.

Consider this. If vacation simply becomes an alternative location to conduct work, at best, how restorative is that? If vacation becomes negotiable, then what is the impact on resilience? At the very least, we need to be aware of our answers or rationalizations.

Resilience researchers[155] have found while traumatic stressors can have a devastating impact on our health, it's "the countless smaller stresses that take a toll" on our bodies. Resilience—"the capacity to successfully adapt to challenges"—is not something that relates solely to the larger issues of life. The small things can bring us down just as well.

Neuroscientist Richard Davidson's research indicates that "the way we cope with little stressors strongly predicts how we'll do once the big stuff hits. Personality is not as big a factor as one might think."[156] Coping depends on the little choices we make.

So, how can we raise our resilience game? How do we train our brains and bodies to cope and bounce back in a healthy manner? Consider the following "Expert Tips for Resilience" as ten places to start:[157]

1. Tap into your core (unshakable) beliefs.
2. Use each stressor as an opportunity to learn.
3. As tough as it might be and as trite and cliché as it might sound, do what you can to remain positive.
4. Learn from a resilient mentor or coach.
5. Don't run away. Confront your challenge (#4 above may be helpful here as is #6 below).
6. Look for and reach out to your support network in difficult times.
7. Keep your brain active and learning new things frequently.
8. Exercise regularly and with discipline.
9. Live in the present—don't ruminate on the past.
10. What trait, characteristic, skill or talent makes you the strong person you are? Give yourself credit for this strength. It is one of your bright spots!

Which point above is one of your strengths? Which is a challenge for you? What resilience plan do you have for the coming week? What is the autobiography you have created for yourself?

Maybe it's time for a revised edition of that story.

Consideration, Conversation, & Collaboration

❦

* Which of the ten points above do you see as part of your community's strengths? Which challenge your community?
* Look at your list of strengths and challenges from the above item. What can your community do to sustain and enhance the strengths? What can you and your neighbors do to make strengths of your challenges?
* Does your community have to wait for adversity to build resilience? Are there strategies, your community members can or do employ before adversity hits to strengthen their grit and resolve?
* What other questions do you need to address regarding this topic?

Meaningful Development[158]

❦

THE END OF EVERY COLLEGE semester brings with it a balance sheet of sorts. What went well? What could have been better?

During my teaching career, I had the opportunity to coordinate faculty development programs on my campus. Thanks to my forward-looking dean and supportive campus president, we slowly and steadily gained traction. Bridges were built and strengthened across our campus. Faculty responded with questions, suggestions, actions, and support. The journey proved to be a professional learning and reaffirming experience. It reminded me of how critical a coherent professional development program can be to any organization in the workplace and in the community. When organized and supported with passion, professional development creates power, vision, and rejuvenation.

The evolution of a team, organization, or community depends on continuous growth. Forward looking leaders understand the importance of continuous growth opportunities for their followers. Development should not be hit or miss—and it should never be considered a *luxury*. The leader must have a plan and that plan must consider the needs of the team members (the individual) as well as the team (the whole) itself.

And, it takes work. Disciplined work. Balanced work. Consider how meaningful professional and personal development can provide a sense of:

1. Bridge building
2. Collaboration
3. Consistency

4. Doing
5. Followership
6. Intentionality
7. Joining the pieces of the puzzle
8. Leadership
9. Listening
10. Perseverance
11. Persistence
12. Humor
13. Reflective practice
14. Support
15. Vision
16. Willingness to fail
17. Willingness to learn from failure
18. Work

Professional and personal growth benefits the community and the people it serves. Just as importantly, the growth can stimulate and sustain personal resilience.

Consideration, Conversation, & Collaboration

~⧏⧐~

* Discuss the 18 items above with a community member. Create two lists. Title one: "Our Community Has a Sense of…." Title the other list: "Our Community Struggles When It Comes to…." From the larger list (18 items), choose the top five for each of your lists. You have identified your strengths and challenges. Add other descriptors if needed.
* Based on your lists above, what is your next step?
* Filmed in Atlantic Beach, FL at sunrise, "Professional Growth and Personal Resilience"[159] gives you a chance to pause, ponder, and breathe.
* What other questions do you need to address regarding this topic?

Meaning & Authenticity[160]

❦

I HAD THE OPPORTUNITY TO listen to Kai Kight at a conference in Austin, Texas. He titled his thoughts "Composing Your World." Using his violin and stories from his journey, he poignantly drove home two oft-repeated life lessons.

1. **Don't regret what might have been.** Kai related how years ago his mother, with tears in her eyes, told him of her breast cancer diagnosis. The tears were not tears of fear, not tears for the unknown or the chemo treatments that lay ahead. No, they were, Kai told the audience, tears for the past. Tears for experiences not lived.

2. **Play your song.** Kai is an accomplished violinist. He can masterfully play the classics. But as he developed his craft he remained restless. He wanted to play his own music. Every opportunity he had, he would construct his own pattern of notes and melodies. These inspired him. The scripted music his conductor led the orchestra through, did not.

Kai's metaphor gives us another powerful reminder to use our precious and limited time to construct and live a life of meaning and authenticity. Rather than shedding tears for an unfulfilled past, embrace the promising present, play your song, and think of the wonderful opportunities in front of you.

A few years ago, I delivered a breakfast keynote to a group of realtors. I encouraged them to evaluate their lives and consider being *responsibly selfish*. That is, I challenged them to take care of their needs. Get to the gym, pick up the musical instrument they always wanted to learn to play, write that novel that was inside of them, or make the difference they can in their communities. Live their authentic lives.

One person in the audience got upset with my message and later sent me an email stating that *selfish* is easy but not good. For me, that is where *responsibly* comes in. Think of it as an *investment* in yourself. It is not license to ignore responsibilities, go into debt because "I deserve [fill in the blank]," or lead a hedonistic lifestyle for the sake of meaningless pleasures.

We all have responsibilities to tend to (children, business, partners, financial obligations, and our own health and well-being, for instance). AND we have an opportunity (obligation?) to experience our lives, embrace the present, and create our own songs.

Consideration, Conversation, & Collaboration

* What *notes* and *melodies* reside within you? What song can you share with the world to make it a better place and you a more complete person?
* What *notes* and *melodies* reside within your community? How does your community encourage and appreciate this *music?* How might it stifle your *song?*
* What song can your community share with the world to make it a better place and its members more complete?
* What other questions do you need to address regarding this topic?

A Deeper Dive: VPEER

❦

For this exercise, focus on two communities with which you have membership. One should be a vibrant and prospering community. The other ranks amongst the weakest. Name each one below.

My strongest community is _____.

My weakest community is _____.

Now, for each community answer the questions below.

- **Visualize** the purpose, journey, and membership of your community. What *weak signals* exist to indicate the future of your community will not look like the past? What does this future focus tell you? What does the community you envision look like?
- **Prioritize** the resources you will need, and the actions required to sustain your community—and make it thrive into the future. What non-negotiable steps do you need to take? What comes first? How will you prioritize **RESILIENCE** to help build and strengthen your community?
- **Exorcise** that which no longer serves or nourishes your community. How can you minimize or eliminate the pernicious effects? Where does this fit with your prioritization of resources and actions? Who will help you identify these factors? Where will this fit in your prioritization?
- **Exercise** and strengthen the emotional, physical, and spiritual dimensions of life. Community building can be challenging work. How will you and your members build and maintain a healthy life style moving forward? Where can you find this on your list of priorities?

* **Realize** your visualization. How often will you stop to evaluate your progress? How will you realize if you are faithfully following the four steps above (visualize, prioritize, exorcise, and exercise)?

Conclusion: No Need To Be An Island

Island: Isolated land. A place of refuge and separation.

ACKNOWLEDGE. ANTICIPATE. APPRECIATE.[161]

As I enjoyed a Bahamian sunrise—disconnected from all but the waves and wind rushing by the ship's balcony—three words came to mind. Acknowledge. Anticipate. Appreciate.

Earlier on that cruise my wife had reminded me of wisdom attributed to Lao Tzu:

> *If you are depressed you are living in the past.*
>
> *If you are anxious you are living in the future.*
>
> *If you are at peace you are living in the present.*

Sage observation, as any of us can choose to be paralyzed by the past, paranoid of the future, or embrace the promise of the present.

We can trap ourselves in the past with ruminations about this, that, and the other. We find ourselves fixated on:

* what did not work well in the last presentation,
* an investment gone bad,
* the vacation from hell,
* the loss of someone special,
* a missed career opportunity,
* the *like* we did not get, or
* a dream never realized.

As we hold on to the past, we miss the present in which we stand, and that will quickly move to the immediate past. Live this way and we obsess on the rear-view mirror. It might serve us better to *acknowledge* what has happened and enjoy a fuller present moment because of lessons learned.

Similarly, it's easy to get trapped in the future as we:

* prepare for the next presentation,
* scrutinize an investment's potential earnings,
* envision a much-needed vacation,
* hope for the end to a traumatic time,
* plan for a career move,
* await the next text, tweet, or post,
* contemplate the direction of a relationship, or
* dream of a better .... [fill in the blank].

Yes, we need to *anticipate* and prepare as best we can for what is on the horizon. But do we need to endlessly rehearse and worry over every little thing that could go wrong at the expense of living the present?

As trite as it may sound, that present moment is the only thing we have. The future cannot be reached without moving through the present. Life happens one moment at a time. If we don't pay attention and appreciate the moments in front and around us, what do we have?

Acknowledge the past. Anticipate the future. And do not forget to appreciate the present. The past is filled with memories, the future holds our hopes, while the present allows for what is.

Consideration, Conversation, & Collaboration

✥ What does your community do to acknowledge its past? Are there particular resources that help with this? Are there relationships that need to be strengthened to improve this historical connection? In what ways can remembering the past help your community live in the present and prepare for the future?

✥ How does your community anticipate the future? Is there a concerted effort to facilitate authentic conversation to identify weak signals about coming trends that will affect you and your neighbors? How does your community keep a positive and all-inclusive future focus as opposed to a fear-based vision?

✥ What resources does your community have to keep people informed about the good things currently happening within the community?

✥ What other questions do you need to address regarding this topic?

Bonus: The Seven-Week Challenge

THE SEVEN RS FOR PURPOSE and growth that this book builds upon is more than just a clever and clichéd mnemonic. The more I have connected with audiences, event planners, friends, neighbors, and family, I have come to view these as core values—the seven areas that guide my life's focus.

Starting as soon as practical, engage in *The Seven-week Challenge for Purpose and Growth* to help your community grow. I have provided a few questions. Change them, tweak them, add to them, and do whatever you need to make this challenge pertinent to your community and its members.

Week 1: RELATIONSHIPS. Which relationship(s) do you need to focus on this week? Which do you need to pay more attention to, strengthen, renew, establish, or minimize? How do you know? Who might be able to help you and your community members? What would you like to accomplish in this area by the end of this week? When will you start?

Week 2: RESOURCES. What assets do you and your community have to help members grow and live with purpose? What assets do you need? Who might be able to help you and your community members? Where do you need to look? How do you know? What would you like to accomplish in this area by the end of this week? When will you start?

Week 3: RELEVANCE. What can you and your neighbors/team members do this week to expose yourselves to experiences, people, and places that are relevant to growth for the members and the community? Who might be able to help you? How do you know? What would you like to accomplish in this area by the end of this week? When will you start?

Week 4: RAINBOWS. What steps will you take this week to move closer to your community dreams? Do you need clarity regarding community goals and direction? How do you know? Who might be able to help you and your neighbors/teammates? What is pulling you and the community toward its dreams? What might be blocking those aspirations? How does it make you feel? What would you like to accomplish in this area by the end of this week? When will you start?

Week 5: REFLECTION. When will you sit and be still so that you can de-clutter your thoughts about your journey? How can you create regular (even if short in duration) moments for you to breathe and disconnect from the world of distractions and noise? Who might be able to help you? How do you know? What would you like to accomplish in this area by the end of this week? When will you start? How can you expand this to the community at large?

Week 6: RESPONSIBILITY. What gentle act of integrity can you commit this week to demonstrate your care and concern for your community and its members? What gentle act of integrity can you commit this week to demonstrate your care and concern for yourself? How can you make or continue to make this a part of your daily work? Who might be able to help you? How do you know? What would you like to accomplish in this area by the end of this week? When will you start?

Week 7: RESILIENCE. What small step can you take this week to help yourself and community members adapt to, learn from, and grow due to adversity? What can you do this week to help strengthen yourself and/or your community for the future? Who might be able to help you? How do you know? What would you like to accomplish in this area by the end of this week? When will you start?

Let me know how you do! (steve@stevepiscitelli.com)

NOTES

1. Steve Piscitelli, (#135) "2012: The Year of Gratitude." December 23, 2012. thegrowthandresiliencenetwork.net/2012/12/23/135-2012-the-year-of-gratitude/.

2. Piscitelli, (#132) "Relevance, Relationships, and Rainbows." December 2, 2012. thegrowthandresiliencenetwork.net/2012/12/02/132-relevance-relationships-and-rainbows/.

3. Working with my dean, John Wall (Florida State College at Jacksonville) toward the end of my college classroom teaching career, we continued to riff and morph on the *Rs* as we developed faculty development programming.

4. September 3, 2018.

5. Piscitelli, (#374) "Can a Community be Inclusive and Like-Minded?" July 23, 2017. thegrowthandresiliencenetwork.net/2017/07/23/374-can-a-community-be-inclusive-and-like-minded/

6. Dan Buettner, *The Blue Zones of Happiness: Lessons from the World's Happiest People*. National Geographic: Washington, DC, 2017. 249-250. Also see, Jean Waak, "The Power of Community: Six Reasons We Need Each Other." Tiny Buddha. No date. tinybuddha.com/blog/6-reasons-we-need-each-other-the-power-of-community/. Accessed July 8, 2018.

7. Norman Cousins, *Anatomy of an Illness as Perceived by the Patient*. New York: W.W. Norton, 1979, 14.

8. Smyre and Richardson, 14. 2016.

9. Piscitelli, (#375) "Capacities for Community Growth and Resilience." July 30, 2017. thegrowthandresiliencenetwork.net/2017/07/30/capacities-for-community-growth-and-resilience/.

10. Alan Gross. Facebook post on the author's Facebook page. July 18, 2017.

11. Smyre, Rick and Neil Richardson. *Preparing for a World that Doesn't Exist—Yet.* Winchester, UK: Change Maker Books, 2016. 14-15.

12. Thank you, Dr. Jeff Hess of Florida State College at Jacksonville.

13. Chip Heath and Dan Heath, *The Power of Moments: Why Certain Experiences Have Extraordinary Impact.* New York: Simon and Schuster, 2017. 18-22.

14. Piscitelli, (#154) "What is Shaping Your Reality?" May 5, 2013. thegrowthandresiliencenetwork.net/2013/05/05/154-what-is-shaping-your-reality/.

15. The blog posts used for this section represent a sampling from my blog *The Growth and Resilience Network®* (thegrowthandresiliencenetwork.net/). Go to it and type into the search box any of the *related terms* found at the top of this section for additional thoughts.

16. Author interview with Billy Hester and Preston Hodges, Jr. Savannah, Georgia. May 9, 2018. Piscitelli, Episode #40, "Community as a Safe Place to Land" on *The Growth and Resilience Network®*, stevepiscitelli.com/media-broadcast/podcast. November, 15, 2018.

17. For more information about the Asbury congregation, visit asburymemorial.org/.

18. Listen to a sermon delivered by the Reverend Billy Hester about vulnerability: www.youtube.com/watch?time_continue=89& v=0YJIKoGNp-o. May 6, 2018.

19. Thanks to the congregant for sharing these words with Preston Hodges, Jr., who in turn shared them with me. If you search the web, you will also find many songs, videos, poems, and books that reference the same wording. Apparently, "a safe place to land" resonates with the soul for many.

20. Piscitelli, (#352) "When Islands Protect and Support." February 19, 2017. thegrowthandresiliencenetwork.net/2017/02/19/352-when-islands-protect-and-support/.

21. The Center for Civil and Human Rights. 100 Ivan Allen, Jr. Blvd. Atlanta, Georgia.

22. Asbury Memorial United Methodist Church. 1008 Henry Street, Savannah, Georgia. asburymemorial.org/history.htm.

23. Piscitelli, (#343) "Reflect, Remove, and Replace. Focus on the Space." December 18, 2016. thegrowthandresiliencenetwork. net/2016/12/18/343-making-filing-and-leaving-the-space/.

24. The National Wellness Institute. *The Six Dimensions of Wellness*. www. nationalwellness.org/?page=Six_Dimensions. No date.

25. Piscitelli, (#251) "Transformational Leadership." March 15, 2015. thegrowthandresiliencenetwork.net/2015/03/15/251-trans-formational-leadership/.

26. Drew Hendricks, "6 Ways to Empower Your Employees with Transformational Leadership." January 27, 2014. *Forbes.com*.

27. Linda A. Hill, et al. "Collective Genius" and "What Does Pixar's Collective Genius Look Like?" *Harvard Business Review.* June 2014 issue. For more information, see the *Harvard Business Review* website.

28. Tony Schwartz, *The Way We're Working Isn't Working: The Four Forgotten Needs that Energize Performance.* Free Press: New York, 2010. 296.

29. Seth Godin, *Leap First: Creating Work That Matters.* Audio book. Boulder, CO: Sounds True, 2015.

30. Piscitelli, "Five Characteristics of an Effective Leader." The Growth and Resilience Network®. https://youtu.be/y06uFDZVDCQ. May 26, 2013.

31. Piscitelli, (#289) "On Making Mistakes, Being Ordinary, and Embracing Growth." December 6, 2015. thegrowthandresiliencenetwork.net/2015/12/06/289-on-making-mistakes-being-ordinary-and-embracing-growth/.

32. Piscitelli, "Episode #2: Transformational Leadership (Part 1)." July 26, 2015. stevepiscitelli.com/media-broadcast/podcast.

33. Brené Brown, *Daring Greatly: How the Courage to be Vulnerable Transforms the Way We Live, Love, Parent, and Lead.* New York: Avery, 2012. Chapter 1.

34. Piscitelli, (#332) "100 Years of Resilience." October 2, 2016. thegrowthandresiliencenetwork.net/2016/10/02/332-100-years-of-resilience/.

35. Piscitelli, stevepiscitelli.com/media-broadcast/podcast. Episode #20: "Life is Not About Me. It's About Others (100 Years of Insight)."

36. Piscitelli, (#319) "Relationships and Leadership." July 3, 2016. the-growthandresiliencenetwork.net/2016/07/03/319-relationships-and-leadership/.

37. Travis Bradberry, "10 Habits of Ultra-Likeable Leaders." *Success Magazine.* June 28, 2016 online issue.

38. James M. Citrin, *The Career Playbook: Essential Advice for Today's Aspiring Young Professional.* New York: Crown, 2015. p. 45.

39. Piscitelli, (#356) "Are You Listening or Adding to the Noise?" March 19, 2017. thegrowthandresiliencenetwork.net/2017/03/19/356-are-you-listening-or-adding-to-the-noise/.

40. Shawn Achor. *Before Happiness.* New York: Crown Business, 2013.

41. Piscitelli, Episode #23. "Listen to Your Heart." *The Growth and Resilience Network*® podcast channel. February 15, 2017. stevepiscitelli.com/media-broadcast/podcast.

42. See note 15 above.

43. For more about the Clara White Mission, visit www.theclarawhitemission.org.

44. Based on an author interview at the Clara White Mission in Jacksonville, Florida, on June 4, 2018. Piscitelli, Episode #43, "Trust as a Core Value" on *The Growth and Resilience Network*®, stevepiscitelli.com/media-broadcast/podcast. February, 15, 2019.

45. Piscitelli, (#174) "We Are All Related." September 22, 2013. thegrowthandresiliencenetwork.net/2013/09/22/174-we-are-all-related/.

46. Piscitelli, "We All Interact in Some Kind of Way—with Reuben Fast Horse." *The Growth and Resilience Network®*. September 21, 2013. youtu.be/-VZvooUy5ns.

47. Piscitelli, (#285) "AreYouRelevant?" November 8, 2015. thegrowthandresiliencenetwork.net/2015/11/08/284-are-you-relevant/.

48. Piscitelli, (#334) "Drive Like Your Kids Lived Here." October 16, 2016. thegrowthandresiliencenetwork.net/2016/10/16/334-drive-like-your-kids-lived-here/.

49. Piscitelli, "Faculty Development: What Important Questions Should We Be Asking?" *The NISOD Papers*. #5. October 2016. www.nisod.org/forms/papers/archive/October2016.pdf.

50. Piscitelli, (#284) "AreYouRelevant?" November 8, 2015. thegrowthandresiliencenetwork.net/2015/11/08/284-are-you-relevant/.

51. See Piscitelli, "Episode #1: Powerful (Mindful) Preparation. Powerful Presentation." *The Growth and Resilience Network®* podcast channel. June 27, 2015. stevepiscitelli.com/media-broadcast/podcast .

52. Bernadette Jiwa, *Meaningful: The Story of Ideas that Fly*. Australia: Perceptive, 2015. Kindle edition.

53. Piscitelli, (#237) "Core Values." December 7, 2014. thegrowthandresiliencenetwork.net/2014/12/07/237-core-values/.

54. Piscitelli, (#327) "Structures for Organization: Implications for Teaching and Learning." August 28, 2016. thegrowthandresiliencenetwork.net/2016/08/28/327-structures-implications-for-teaching-and-training/.

55. Ken Bain, *What the Best College Teachers Do.* Harvard UP, 2004.

56. Heath and Heath, Chapter 4.

57. Piscitelli. "Structures of Organization (A Teaching and Learning Model)." The Growth and Resilience Network®. https://youtu.be/ EQWAH_dibJE. August 26, 2016.

58. Piscitelli, (#254) "The Five Ps of New Employee Mentoring." April 5, 2015. thegrowthandresiliencenetwork.net/2015/04/05/254-the- five-ps-of-new-employee-mentoring/.

59. Piscitelli, (#298) "Do You Have 'Hell, Yeah!' Goals?" February, 7, 2016. thegrowthandresiliencenetwork.net/2016/02/07/298-do- you-have-hell-yeah-goals/.

60. Piscitelli, "Episode #12. Entrepreneurship: The Art of Intentionality, Growth, and Resilience." *The Growth and Resilience Network®* podcast channel. March 15, 2016. stevepiscitelli.com/media-broadcast/ podcast.

61. Derek Sivers, *Anything You Want: 40 Lessons for a New Kind of Entrepreneur.* New York: Random House, 2015. Kindle edition.

62. Piscitelli, (#226) "Kaizen: Movement Toward Improvement." September 21, 2014. thegrowthandresiliencenetwork.net/2014/ 09/21/226-kaizen-movement-toward-improvement/.

63. See note 15 above.

64. Face-to-face interview with Gloria Niec, Mary Pat Rosenthal, and Eileen Crawford of the Celebration Foundation's *Thriving In Place* initiative. July 13, 2018. Piscitelli, Episode #41, "Relationships as

a Community's Most Important Resource" on *The Growth and Resilience Network®*, stevepiscitelli.com/media-broadcast/podcast. December, 15, 2018. Also, visit celebrationfoundation.org/ for more information. I had the honor to host a question and answer session with members during their weekly luncheon (July 13, 2018). Some of their responses contributed to this story.

65. Celebration Foundation. "New Urbanism." celebrationfoundation. org/what-we-do/new-urbanism/. Accessed July 16, 2018.

66. See post "RESOURCES: 3.2" for more information on this point.

67. High school students volunteer for various activities, such as serving and helping at the weekly luncheon.

68. Piscitelli, (#359) "Collisions and Serendipity." April 9, 2017. the-growthandresiliencenetwork.net/2017/04/09/359-collisions-and-serendipity/.

69. To hear or read about Tony Hsieh's vision of collisions, type his name and *collisions* into your favorite search engine for more information. Also, see his book *Delivering Happiness: A Path to Profits, Passion, and Purpose*. New York: Business Plus, 2010.

70. Piscitelli, (#414) "Come Together." April 29, 2018. thegrowthandre-siliencenetwork.net/2018/04/29/414-come-together-food-friends-and-family/.

71. Buettner, 80-81.

72. Kevin M. Kniffin, et al. "Eating Together at the Firehouse: How Workplace Commensality Relates to the Performance of Firefighters." September 18, 2015. Accessed July 11, 2018. www.ncbi.nlm.nih.gov/

pmc/articles/PMC4864863/?utm_source=Broken+Brain&utm_campaign=b6f13872c5-EMAIL_CAMPAIGN_2018_03_29&utm_medium=email&utm_term=0_e9a7b3b4f1-b6f13872c5-114698789&mc_cid=b6f13872c5&mc_eid=3bf49479a3.

73. Julianne Holt-Lunstad, et al. "Social Relationships and Mortality Risk: A Meta-analytic Review." July 27, 2010/ journals.plos.org/plosmedicine/article?id=10.1371/journal.pmed.1000316.

74. 74 George E. Vaillant, et al. "The Study of Adult Development." An article about the study can be found on Harvard.edu: Liz Mineo, *The Harvard Gazette.* "Good Genes Are Nice, But Joy Is Better." April 2017.

75. Piscitelli, (#305) "Listen. Question. Grow." March 27, 2016. thegrowthandresiliencenetwork.net/2016/03/27/305-listen-question-grow/.

76. Piscitelli, "Episode #14: Overcoming Adversity among Disabled Clients with Prader-Willi Syndrome." *The Growth and Resilience Network®* podcast channel. May 15, 2016. stevepiscitelli.com/media-broadcast/podcast.

77. Marilee Adams. *Change Your Questions Change Your Life (3rd ed.).* San Francisco: Berrett-Koehler, 2015.

78. I wrote and recorded a tongue-in-cheek song titled "I'm Gonna Should on You" aimed at all those who *should on* us. Steve Piscitelli, *Find Your Happy Place!* 2010. stevepiscitelli.com/media-broadcast/music.

79. Piscitelli, (#363) "A Resiliency Group: Collaboration, Creativity, Caring, and Collegiality." May 7, 2017. thegrowthandresiliencenetwork.net/2017/05/07/4404/.

80. Olivia Waxman, "Napping Around: Colleges Provide Campus Snooze Rooms." *Time.com.* August 29, 2014.

81. Email correspondence with Tony Ferrara of Zappos. April 12, 2017.

82. Piscitelli, (#290) "Life Fitness and Mental Discipline." December 13, 2015. thegrowthandresiliencenetwork.net/2015/12/13/290-physical-fitness-and-mental-discipline/.

83. Piscitelli, (#130) "Making Your Life Work." *The Growth and Resilience Network®.* November 18, 2012. thegrowthandresiliencenetwork. net/2012/11/18/130-making-your-life-work/.

84. Piscitelli, "Episode #9: Physical Fitness and Mental Discipline." *The Growth and Resilience Network®* podcast channel. December 15, 2015. stevepiscitelli.com/media-broadcast/podcast.

85. Piscitelli, (#297) "In Their Words: Leadership and Collaboration." January 31, 2016. thegrowthandresiliencenetwork.net/2016/01/31/297-in-their-words-leadership-and-collaboration/.

86. February 2016.

87. Piscitelli, (#431) "Pay Attention to the 360° View." August 26, 2018. thegrowthandresiliencenetwork.net/2018/08/26/431-pay-attention-to-the-360-view/.

88. Piscitelli, (#196) "On Collegiality and Collaboration: Reflections from San Diego." February 23, 2014. thegrowthandresiliencenetwork.net/2014/02/23/195-on-collegiality-and-collaboration-reflections-from-san-diego/.

89. See note 15 above.

90. C.R. Snyder, *Handbook of Hope: Theory, Measures, and Applications.* Academic: San Diego, 2000. 8-12.

91. Piscitelli, Episode #44, "Mentors for Music, Hope, and Rainbows" on *The Growth and Resilience Network®*, stevepiscitelli.com/media-broadcast/podcast. March, 15, 2019.

92. Dalton Cyr. www.daltoncyr.com/. Check out his award-winning trilogy "Breathe" bit.ly/DCyrBreatheTrilogy. Here is the video of Dalton signing and picking guitar with me on my song, "I Wanna Be a Kid Again," when Dalton was a younger picker youtu. be/2EYddxKaVEY, November 8, 2010.

93. Izzy Moon Mayforth, "It Rained Today." 2015.

94. Piscitelli, (#398) "We Are Where We Are." January 7, 2018. thegrowthandresiliencenetwork. net/2018/01/07/398-we-are-where-we-are/.

95. Marcel Schwantes, "Richard Branson Says You Should Do Three Things to Achieve More Happiness in 2018." *Inc.com.* January 2, 2018.

96. Piscitelli, (#253) "Bridging the Gap: What Stories Are You Telling Yourself?" March 29, 2015. thegrowthandresiliencenet-work.net/2015/03/29/253-bridging-the-gap-the-stories-we-tell-ourselves-and-the-stories-we-live/.

97. Piscitelli, (#355) "Go-Go or No-Go?" March 12, 2017. thegrowthan-dresiliencenetwork.net/2017/03/12/4326/. Also see, Piscitelli, (#21) "Goals, Failure, and Choosing to Move Forward." October 17, 2010. thegrowthandresiliencenetwork.net/2010/10/17/goals-failure-and-choosing-to-move-forward/.

98. Angela Ahrendts, "A Letter to my Daughters: Always Be Present." March 7, 2017. LinkedIn.com

99. I created a video metaphor demonstrating these three types. You can find it on my YouTube channel at youtu.be/GGYikTg4fx8. December 22, 2017.

100. Shawn Achor, *Before Happiness: The Five Hidden Keys to Achieving Success, Spreading Happiness, and Sustaining Positive Change.* New York: Crown Business, 2013.

101. Piscitelli, (#376) "The Lesson from the Bunny and the Deer." August 6, 2017. thegrowthandresiliencenetwork. net/2017/08/06/376-the-lesson-of-the-bunny-and-the-deer/.

102. Piscitelli, (#91) "Success Strategies for the Classroom and the Business World." February 19, 2012. thegrowthandresiliencenetwork.net/2012/02/19/success-strategies-for-the-classroom-and-the-business-world/.

103. Piscitelli, *Study Skills: Do I Really Need This Stuff,* 3rd edition. Boston: Pearson, 2013, pages 154-155.

104. Piscitelli, (#432) "Compassion." September 2, 2018. thegrowthandresiliencenetwork.net/2018/09/02/432-compassion/.

105. Piscitelli, "Study Skills: Success Strategies for the Classroom." The Growth and Resilience Network®. February 13, 2012.

106. Piscitelli, (#271) "Comfort Zone." August 2, 2015. thegrowthandresiliencenetwork.net/2015/08/02/272-comfort-zone/.

107. Piscitelli, (#99) "Dreams: Remaining Open to the Possibilities." April 15, 2012. thegrowthandresiliencenetwork.net/2012/04/15/ dreams-remaining-open-to-the-possibilities/.

108. See note 15 above.

109. Personal conversation. May 24, 2018. Jacksonville, Florida. Piscitelli, Episode #42, "Helping a Village Find Its Voice" on *The Growth and Resilience Network®*, stevepiscitelli.com/media-broadcast/ podcast. January 15, 2019. Also, see their website at ntszjax.org/.

110. Piscitelli, "(#155) Staying Focused on Your Dream." *The Growth and Resilience Network®.* thegrowthandresiliencenetwork.net/ 2013/05/12/155-staying-focused-on-your-dream/. May 12, 2013.

111. Piscitelli, (#216) "Value-Driven Actions: What Guides Your Life?" July 13, 2014. thegrowthandresiliencenetwork. net/2014/07/13/216-value-driven-actions/.

112. Piscitelli, "Your Effort Matters: Thank You!" The Growth and Resilience Network®. January 18, 2016. Filmed at San Jacinto College, Pasadena, Texas.

113. Piscitelli, (#215) "Consistent Talk or Consistent Action?" July 6, 2014. thegrowthandresiliencenetwork.net/2014/07/06/215- consistent-talk-or-consistent-action/.

114. Jim Collins, *Good to Great: Why Some Companies Make the Leap...and Others Don't.* New York: HarperBusiness, 2001, 202-210.

115. Piscitelli, (#227) "Action." September 28, 2014. thegrowthandre- siliencenetwork.net/2014/09/28/227-action/.

116. Ruffalo Noel Levitz, "2017 National Freshman Motivation to Complete College Report." 2017, 8. learn.ruffalonl.com/rs/395-EOG-977/images/2017_NationalFreshman_Motivation_to_Complete.pdf.

117. See Michael A. Singer, *The Untethered Soul: The Journey Beyond Yourself.* California: New Harbinger Publications, Inc., 2007. Chapter 9, "Removing Your Inner Thorn" might provide material to consider on why we act as we do. Awareness can help us question assumptions.

118. Piscitelli, "Awareness, Assumptions, and Actions: Why You Do What You Do? TEDx. https://youtu.be/HZQ2GEhoWYs. November 3, 2014.

119. Piscitelli, (#194) "Matching Words to Action." February 2, 2014. thegrowthandresiliencenetwork.net/2014/02/02/193-matching-words-to-action/. Seth Godin speaks of "cogs" (faceless characters following someone else's script) and "linchpins" (the people who lead and make a difference) in his book *Linchpin: Are You Indispensable?* New York: Portfolio/Penguin, 2010, vi; 1-6.

120. Piscitelli, (#270) "Have You Spent Time with Ida Only?" July 26, 2015. thegrowthandresiliencenetwork.net/2015/07/26/270-have-you-spent-time-with-ida-ownly/.

121. Piscitelli, (#87) "Priority Management: Are You Doing the Right Things or Are You Just Doing Stuff?" January 22, 2012. thegrowthandresiliencenetwork.net/2012/01/22/priority-management-are-you-doing-the-right-things-or-are-you-just-doing-stuff/.

122. Piscitelli, "Priority Management: Are You Doing the Right Things or Are You Just Doing Stuff?" The Growth and Resilience Network®. https://youtu.be/QmMUy2t0ZvQ. January 18, 2012.

123. Piscitelli, (#400) "Do We Live in a Post-Fact World?" January 21, 2018. thegrowthandresiliencenetwork.net/2018/01/21/4878/.

124. See note 15 above.

125. Piscitelli, Episode #45, "Someone Has to Be the Grownup in the Room" on *The Growth and Resilience Network®*, stevepiscitelli.com/media-broadcast/podcast. April 15, 2019.

126. Piscitelli, (#24) "Words for Reflection," November 7, 2010, thegrowthandresiliencenetwork.net/2010/11/07/words-for-reflection/.

127. The quote appears in various forms. I have seen *system* replaced by *organization, program, college,* and *course.* You can find attribution to W. Edwards Deming, Paul Batalden, Donald Berwick, and Byron McClenny. Google the phrase to find various sources and contexts for the quote.

128. Piscitelli, (#183) "Now Is My Time." November 24, 2013. thegrowthandresiliencenetwork.net/2013/11/24/183-now-is-my-time/.

129. Piscitelli, (#323) "Who Sets Your Agenda?" July 31, 2016. thegrowthandresiliencenetwork.net/2016/07/31/323-who-sets-your-agenda/.

130. McCombs, Maxwell E. and Donald L. Shaw, "The Agenda-Setting Function of Mass Media." *The Public Opinion Quarterly*, v. 36, n.2. Summer 1972. 176-187.

131. Bakari Akil II, "Who Is Setting Your Agenda." *Psychology Today.* October 31, 2009. Found on *Psychology Today.com.*

132. Piscitelli, (#329) "Textured, Color, and a Bit Off-Center." September 11, 2016. thegrowthandresiliencenetwork.net/2016/09/11/329-textured-colored-and-a-bit-off-center/.

133. Piscitelli, (#422) "Ask. Listen. Act." June 24, 2018. thegrowthandresiliencenetwork.net/2018/06/24/422-ask-listen-act/.

134. Gino Wickman, *Traction: Get a Grip on Your Business.* Dallas: BenBella Books, 2011.

135. Piscitelli, "Feeding Your Mind. Creating Your Life." The Growth and Resilience Network®. https://youtu.be/FLHajlF6RLE. December 31, 2011.

136. Piscitelli, (#194) "Honor the Past. Celebrate the Present. Embrace the Future." February 9, 2014. thegrowthandresiliencenetwork.net/2014/02/09/194-honor-the-past-celebrate-the-present-embrace-the-future/.

137. See "Interview with Steve Piscitelli, Scholar in Residence." February 4, 2014. www.youtube.com/watch?v=IziAvOsSBdc.

138. Piscitelli, (#244) "Do You Have Your Own Board of Directors?" January 25, 2015. thegrowthandresiliencenetwork.net/2015/01/25/244-do-you-have-your-own-board-of-directors/.

139. Piscitelli, "Do You Have Your Own Board of Directors." The Growth and Resilience Network®. https://youtu.be/XY2Kp384xEw. January 24, 2015.

140. See note 15 above.

141. Piscitelli, Episode #39, "Facing the Worst. Preparing for the Best." on *The Growth and Resilience Network®*, https://stevepiscitelli.com/media-broadcast/podcast. October, 15, 2018.

142. Bobbi de Cordova-Hanks and Jerry Hanks, *Tears of Joy*. Pennsylvania: Infinity, 2006.

143. Piscitelli, (#394) "Resilience: Supporting, Flourishing, Growing." December 10, 2017. thegrowthandresiliencenetwork.net/2017/12/10/394-a-few-thoughts-and-questions-about-resilience/.

144. Hara Estroff Marano, "The Art of Resilience." *Psychology Today*. June 9, 2016. Found on *Psychology Today.com*.

145. Piscitelli, (#71) "Hit the Reset Button." October 2, 2011. thegrowthandresiliencenetwork.net/2011/10/02/hit-the-reset-button/.

146. Wayne Dyer won international acclaim as an author and philosopher. You can read more about him, his inspirational thoughts, and books at WayneDyer.com.

147. Piscitelli, (#98) "Fitness: A Better Version of Me." April 8, 2012. thegrowthandresiliencenetwork.net/2012/04/08/fitness-a-better-version-of-me/.

148. Piscitelli, "Fitness: A Better Version of Me." The Growth and Resilience Network®. https://youtu.be/vJ2AgzcTI4k. March 21, 2012.

149. Piscitelli, (#336) "Wellbeing is a Skill: From Balance to Integration." October 30, 2016. thegrowthandresiliencenetwork.net/2016/10/30/336-wellbeing-is-a-skill/.

150. Shana Lynch, "Why Your Workplace Might Be Killing You?" *Insights by Stanford Business*. The Graduate School of Stanford

Business. February 23, 2015. www.gsb.stanford.edu/insights/
why-your-workplace-might-be-killing-you.

151. Michael Moon, "Move Over, Wellness. Creating an Engaged
Culture through Wellbeing." *Virgin Pulse.* Found on VirginPulse.
com.

152. Piscitelli, *Rhythms of College Success.* Upper Saddle River, NJ:
Pearson. 2008. 18.

153. Piscitelli, (#262) "Resilience: What's Your Story?" May 31, 2015.
thegrowthandresiliencenetwork.net/2015/05/31/262-resilience/.

154. Jack, Dickey, "Save the American Vacation." *Time.* May 21, 2015.
46-49.

155. Mandy Oaklander, "The Science of Bouncing Back." *Time.* May
21, 2015, 34-42.

156. Oaklander, 40.

157. Oaklander, 42.

158. Piscitelli, (#239) "Reflecting on Meaningful Professional
Development." December 21, 2014. thegrowthandresiliencenet-
work.net/2014/12/21/239-reflecting-on-meaningful-profession-
al-development/.

159. Piscitelli, "Professional Growth and Personal Resilience." The
GrowthandResilienceNetwork®. https://youtu.be/38tTPCZGK-4.
December 19, 2014.

160. Piscitelli, (#315) "Play Your Song, Now." June 5, 2016. thegrowthandresiliencenetwork.net/2016/06/05/315-play-your-song-now/.

161. Piscitelli, (#395) "Acknowledge. Anticipate. Appreciate." December 17, 2017. thegrowthandresiliencenetwork.net/2017/12/17/395-acknowledge-anticipate-appreciate/.

WORKS CITED

"40 Developmental Assets® for Adolescents (ages 12-18)." The Search Institute®. 1997, 2006. www.search-institute.org. Accessed July 8, 2018.

Achor, Shawn. *Before Happiness: The Five Hidden Keys to Achieving Success, Spreading Happiness, and Sustaining Positive Change.* New York: Crown Business, 2013.

Adams, Marilee. *Change Your Questions Change Your Life (3rd ed.).* San Francisco: Berrett-Koehler, 2015.

Ahrendts, Angela. "A Letter to My Daughters: Always Be Present." March 7, 2017. Published on LinkedIn.com.

Akil II, Bakari. "Who is Setting Your Agenda." *Psychology Today.* October 31, 2009. The article was found on *Psychology Today.com.*

Alinsky, Saul. *Rules for Radicals.* New York: Vintage Books edition, 1989.

Asbury Memorial United Methodist Church. Savannah, Georgia. http://asburymemorial.org/history.htm.

Bain, Ken. *What the Best College Teachers Do.* Harvard University Press, 2004.

Bradberry, Travis. "10 Habits of Ultra-Likeable Leaders." *Success Magazine.* June 28, 2016. Online issue.

Brown, Brené. *Daring Greatly: How the Courage to be Vulnerable Transforms the Way We Live, Love, Parent, and Lead.* New York: Avery, 2012. Chapter 1.

Buettner, Dan. *The Blue Zones of Happiness: Lessons from the World's Happiest People.* Washington, D.C: National Geographic, 2017. Celebration Foundation. Celebration, Florida. https://celebrationfoundation.org.

The Center for Civil and Human Rights. 100 Ivan Allen, Jr. Blvd. Atlanta, Georgia. https://www.civilandhumanrights.org/.

Choosing to Move Forward." October 17, 2010. https://thegrowthan-dresiliencenetwork.net/2010/10/17/goals-failure-and-choosing-to-move-forward/.

Collins, Jim. *Good to Great: Why Some Companies Make the Leap...and Others Don't.* New York: HarperBusiness, 2001.

Citrin, James. *The Career Playbook: Essential Advice for Today's Aspiring Young Professional.* (Kindle edition). New York: Crown Business, 2015.

The Clara White Mission. www.theclarawhitemission.org.

Cleary, Thomas. *No Barrier: Unlocking the Zen Koan.* New York: Bantam Books, 1993.

Cousins, Norman. *Anatomy of an Illness as Perceived by the Patient.* New York: W.W. Norton,1979.

Cyr, Dalton. http://www.daltoncyr.com/

de Cordova-Hanks, Bobbi, and Jerry Hanks, *Tears of Joy.* (Kindle edi-tion). Infinity Publishing: Pennsylvania, 2006.

Dickey, Jack. "Save the American Vacation." *Time.* May 21, 2015. 46-49.

Godin, Seth. *Leap First: Creating Work that Matters.* Audio book. Boulder, CO: Sounds True, 2015.

Gross, Alan. Post on the author's Facebook page. July 18, 2017.

Heath, Chip and Dan Heath, *The Power of Moments: Why Certain Experiences Have Extraordinary Impact.* New York: Simon and Schuster, 2017.

Hendricks, Drew. "6 Ways to Empower Your Employees with Transformational Leadership." January 27, 2014. *Forbes.com.*

Hill, Linda A., et al. "Collective Genius." *Harvard Business Review.* June 2014. *Harvard Business Review website.*

---. "What Does Pixar's Collective Genius Look Like?" *Harvard Business Review.* June 11, 2014. *Harvard Business Review* website.

Holt-Lunstad, Julianne, et al. "Social Relationships and Mortality Risk: A Meta-analytic Review." July 27, 2010. http://journals.plos.org/plosmedicine/article?id=10.1371/journal.pmed.1000316. Accessed July 11, 2018.

Hsieh, Tony. *Delivering Happiness: A Path to Profits, Passion, and Purpose.* New York: Business Plus, 2010.

"Interview with Steve Piscitelli, Scholar in Residence." February 4, 2014. https://www.youtube.com/watch?v=IziAvOsSBdc.

Jiwa, Bernadette. *Meaningful: The Story of Ideas that Fly.* Australia: Perceptive Press, 2015. Kindle edition.

Kniffin, Kevin M., et al. "Eating Together at the Firehouse: How Workplace Commensality Relates to the Performance of Firefighters." September 18, 2015. Accessed July 11, 2018. https://www.ncbi.nlm.nih.gov/pmc/articles/PMC4864863/?utm_source=Broken+Brain&utm_campaign=b6f13872c5-EMAIL_CAMPAIGN_2018_03_29&utm_medium=email&utm_term=0_e9a7b3b4f1-b6f13872c5-114698789&mc_cid=b6f13872c5&mc_eid=3bf49479a3

Lynch, Shana. "Why Your Workplace Might Be Killing You?" *Insights by Stanford Business.* The Graduate School of Stanford Business. February 23, 2015. https://www.gsb.stanford.edu/insights/why-your-workplace-might-be-killing-you.

Marano, Estroff Hara. "The Art of Resilience." *Psychology Today.* June 9, 2016. The article was found on PsychologyToday.com.

Mayforth, Izzy Moon. "It Rained Today." 2015.

McCombs, Maxwell E., and Donald L. Shaw, "The Agenda-Setting Function of Mass Media." *The Public Opinion Quarterly*, v. 36, n.2. Summer 1972. 176-187.

McKnight, John, and Peter Block. *The Abundant Community: Awakening the Power of Families and Neighborhoods.* San Francisco: Berrett-Koehler Publishers, Inc., 2012.

Moon, Michael. "Move Over, Wellness. Creating an Engaged Culture through Wellbeing." *Virgin Pulse.* Found on VirginPulse.com. The National Wellness Institute. *The Six Dimensions of Wellness.* http://www.nationalwellness.org/?page=Six_Dimensions. No date.

New Town Success Zone. http://ntszjax.org/.

Oaklander, Mandy. "The Science of Bouncing Back." *Time.* May 21, 2015. 34-42.

Piscitelli, Steve. *The Growth and Resilience Network®* (blog). This book has excerpts from more than fifty posts from this blog. Specific references can be found in the Endnotes of this book. To access the site, go to https://thegrowthandresiliencenetwork.net/.

---. *The Growth and Resilience Network®* (podcast channel). This book references episodes from this channel. Specific references can be found in the Endnotes of this book. To access the full catalog of podcast episodes, go to https://stevepiscitelli.com/media-broadcast/podcast.

---. "I Wanna Be a Kid Again" (video). https://youtu.be/2EYddxKaVEY, November 8, 2010.

---. "Three Cups of Water: A Metaphor for Resilience and Much More." https://youtu.be/GGYikTg4fx8. December 22, 2017.

Ruffalo Noel Levitz. "National Freshman Motivation to Complete College Reports." No date. https://www.ruffalonl.com/papers-research-higher-education-fundraising/student-retention-white-papers-and-trend-reports/national-freshman-attitudes-reports.

Schwantes, Marcel. "Richard Branson Says You Should Do Three Things to Achieve More Happiness in 2018." *Inc.* January 2, 2018.

Schwartz, Tony. *The Way We're Working Isn't Working: The Four Forgotten Needs that Energize Performance*. Free Press: New York, 2010.

Singer, Michael A. *The Untethered Soul: The Journey Beyond Yourself.* California: New Harbinger Publications, Inc., 2007.

Sivers, Derek. *Anything You Want: 40 Lessons for a New Kind of Entrepreneur.* New York: Random House, 2015. Kindle edition.

Smyre, Rick and Neil Richardson. *Preparing for a World that Doesn't Exist—Yet.* Winchester, UK: Change Maker Books, 2016.

Snyder, C.R. *Handbook of Hope: Theory, Measures, and Applications.* San Diego: Academic Press, 2000. 8-12.

Vaillant, George E., et al. "The Study of Adult Development." An article about the study can be found on Harvard.edu: Liz Mineo, *The Harvard Gazette*. "Good Genes Are Nice, But Joy Is Better." April 2017.

Waak, Jean. "The Power of Community: Six Reasons We Need Each Other." Tiny Buddha. No date. https://tinybuddha.com/blog/6-reasons-we-need-each-other-the-power-of-community/. Accessed July 8, 2018.

Waxman, Olivia. "Napping Around: Colleges Provide Campus Snooze Rooms." *Time*. August 29, 2014. Found on Time.com

Wickman, Gino. *Traction: Get a Grip on Your Business*. Dallas: BenBella Books. 2011.